Python and Machine Learning For Kids

A Must-Have Coding Guide
For Parents and Teachers

Igor Balk

This book is dedicated to Marina, my pillar of support, and to Daniel, the first to bravely test the methodology detailed within. Marina, your unfaltering help has been invaluable in this endeavor. Daniel, your curiosity has shaped the techniques shared here. Thank you both for being part of this journey into the realms of machine learning and Python.

Table of Contents

INTRODUCTION

Welcome to "Python and Machine Learning for Kids," a comprehensive resource meticulously designed for young learners, educators, and parents. This book was born out of the innovative curriculum taught at the esteemed Machine Learning For Kids (ML4K) school, located in Lexington, Massachusetts. The ML4K approach was created by an outstanding group of MIT alumni, who believed in the importance of empowering the next generation with the knowledge of Python and machine learning.

Our book brings to the forefront MIT's time-honored ethos of "Mens et Manus," or "Mind and Hand." In keeping with this credo, the methodology we adopt throughout this book is one of "learning by doing." The content is scaffolded in a way that children not only understand theoretical concepts, but they also actively engage in hands-on programming tasks that bring these theories to life.

Starting from the rudimentary basics of Python programming, we journey through the complexities of data structures, control flow, and functions. We then embark on the captivating world of machine learning, with engaging lessons on data visualization, data manipulation using the pandas library, and exploring various machine learning algorithms.

The book features practical, real-world projects, where students apply their understanding and skills. From data sets such as the Titanic disaster and mobile phone prices to fun programming projects like developing a Tic Tac Toe game, the projects are sure to excite and engage our young coders.

Each lesson is thoughtfully structured, with clear objectives, lesson plans, descriptions, and detailed notes to foster understanding and aid in the reinforcement of concepts. This allows students to progress at their own pace, steadily building on their knowledge base, and gaining confidence in their programming and data science skills.

It's important to note that the lessons presented in this book are structured as distinct chapters, each focusing on a specific topic or set of related concepts. These chapters provide logical partitions of information, aiding in systematic learning. However, they may not precisely correspond to the real-world class lessons conducted at "Machine Learning for Kids" school or any other educational setting. The time it takes to complete a chapter can vary depending on the complexity of the topic, the learner's prior knowledge, and their pace of learning. Therefore, while these chapters can certainly be used as a guideline for structuring class lessons, educators are encouraged to adapt and divide the content based on their students' needs, capabilities, and the time constraints of their particular teaching scenario. Flexibility is key in creating an effective and engaging learning experience.

While this book aims to impart Python and machine learning skills to young learners, it is also a resource for parents and educators. It is a tool to foster a love for coding and data science in children, and also serves as a guide for teachers and parents to support the children's learning journey.

As we take the plunge into the world of Python and machine learning, let us bear in mind that our ultimate goal is to stimulate curiosity, encourage critical thinking, and nurture problem-solving abilities in our young learners. This aligns with the MIT's principle of "learning by doing" and brings the spirit of "Mens et Manus" into each lesson.

So, let's embark on this exciting adventure together, instilling in our future generation the spirit of inquiry, the joy of discovery, and the thrill of problem-solving – one line of code at a time.

Let's get coding!

SETTING UP THE TECHNOLOGY AND GATHERING DATA

Let's familiarize ourselves with the key technologies we will use throughout this book. We'll also guide you through the process of acquiring important datasets, which will play a pivotal role in many of our lessons.

Our programming and machine learning exercises require an environment conducive to experimentation and learning. To that end, we highly recommend using Google Colaboratory, commonly known as Google Colab. It is a cloud-based Python development environment that allows real-time collaboration, making it an ideal tool for the classroom setting.

Moreover, Google Colab offers the advantage of freeing us from worrying about the underlying system configuration. It requires no setup, runs entirely in the cloud, and most importantly, it enables you to write and execute Python code through your browser. This makes it an accessible and practical solution for educators and students alike.

As each student will be writing and testing their own Python scripts, we advise creating individual Google accounts for each student. This will allow them to have their own workspace and enable them to save their work independently. It encourages a sense of ownership, organization, and responsibility towards their work.

Moving on to the data that we'll be using: real-world data brings abstract concepts to life, providing context and making the learning process more engaging. For this purpose, we will be utilizing several open-source datasets from Kaggle, a platform that hosts a multitude of datasets in diverse domains. We will provide specific references in each chapter to guide you on which datasets to download from Kaggle.

Finally, let's turn our attention to a unique exercise we'll embark on in this chapter: creating our own datasets!

Specifically, we'll learn how to scrape Wikipedia pages to create two exciting datasets – 'Olympic Medals' and 'World Population.' This exercise will not only give you a sneak peek into how data is gathered in real-world scenarios but also provide us with the data resources we'll need for subsequent lessons.

Web scraping is a valuable skill that involves extracting information from websites. By scraping Wikipedia pages, we'll compile information about Olympic Medals and World Population into structured datasets, which we can then use for our coding and machine learning tasks.

So, get ready to roll up your sleeves as we dive into setting up our technological environment, sourcing datasets, and even creating our own. It's going to be an exciting ride!

Remember, the journey of a thousand miles begins with a single step. Let's take that step together, equipping ourselves with the right tools and data, as we set out on this enriching journey into the realms of Python and machine learning. Onward!

Gather the Data:

Use the following code to download list of Olympic medals from Wikipedia page and save it to csv file. The following Python code snippet uses the BeautifulSoup library to scrape the medal data from the provided Wikipedia page[1] and saves it to a CSV file named "Medals.csv".:

PYTHON CODE

```python
import csv
import requests
import re
from bs4 import BeautifulSoup

# This function scrapes medal data from a Wikipedia page
def download_medal_data(url):
    # Send a GET request to the given URL
    response = requests.get(url)
    # Raise an exception if the request was
    unsuccessful
    response.raise_for_status()
    # Parse the HTML content of the page
    soup = BeautifulSoup(response.content, 'html.parser')
    # Find the specific table that contains the medal data
    table = soup.find('table', class_='wikitable sortable')
    # Create a dictionary to store the medal counts per country
    medal_count = {}
```

---

1 https://en.wikipedia.org/wiki/All-time_Olympic_Games_medal_table

```python
# Find all the table rows
rows = table.find_all('tr')
# Loop over each row, skipping the header row
for row in rows[1:]:
    # Find all cells in the row
    cells = row.find_all('td')
    # Ensure the row has enough cells
    if len(cells) >= 5:
        # Clean the country name by removing
        # bracketed and parenthesized content
        country = re.sub(r'\[[^]]*\]|\([^)]*\)', '',
        cells[0].text.strip())
        # Initialize the medal count
        medals = 0

        # Try to convert each cell's content to an int
        # (after stripping commas) and add it to the medal count
        # If the conversion fails, ignore that cell
        try:
            medals += int(cells[1].text.strip().
            replace(',', ''))
        except ValueError:
            pass
        try:
            medals += int(cells[2].text.strip().replace(',', ''))
        except ValueError:
            pass
        try:
            medals += int(cells[3].text.strip().replace(',', ''))
        except ValueError:
            pass
```

```python
    # If both country and medals values are
    # present, store them in the dictionary
    if country and medals:
        medal_count[country.strip()] =
        medal_count.get(country.strip(), 0) + medals

# Return the dictionary of medal counts
return medal_count


# This function saves medal data to a CSV file
def save_to_csv(data, filename):
    # Convert the dictionary to a list of tuples
    rows = [(country, count) for country, count in data.items()]
    # Sort the rows by country name
    sorted_rows = sorted(rows, key=lambda x: x[0])

    # Open the CSV file in write mode
    with open(filename, 'w', newline='', encoding='utf-8') as file:
        writer = csv.writer(file)
        # Write the header row
        writer.writerow(['Country', 'Medals'])
        # Write the data rows
        writer.writerows(sorted_rows)


# This is the main entry point of the script
if __name__ == '__main__':
    # Define the URL of the Wikipedia page
    url = 'https://en.wikipedia.org/wiki/All-time_Olympic_Games_
medal_table'
    # Download the medal data from the page
    medal_data = download_medal_data(url)
    # Save the medal data to a CSV file
    save_to_csv(medal_data, 'Medals.csv')
```

Running the code will scrape the medal data from the provided Wikipedia page and save it to a CSV file named "Medals.csv" in the same directory as the Python script. The download_medal_data function scrapes a Wikipedia page for medal count data, cleans the country names and adds up the medal counts. The save_to_csv function saves this data to a CSV file.

The following Python code that downloads population data by country from the Wikipedia page and saves it to a CSV file named "Population.csv".:

PYTHON CODE

```python
# Import necessary modules
import csv
import requests
from bs4 import BeautifulSoup

# Define a function to download population data
def download_population_data(url):
    # Send a GET request to the given URL
    response = requests.get(url)
    # Check if request was successful, else raise exception
    response.raise_for_status()
    # Parse the HTML content of the page using BeautifulSoup
    soup = BeautifulSoup(response.content, 'html.parser')
    # Find the table containing the population data
    table = soup.find('table', class_='wikitable sortable')
```

```python
# Initialize list with headers for our data
data = [['Country', 'Population']]

# Get all table rows
rows = table.find_all('tr')
# Loop over each row, starting from second row
(skipping headers)
for row in rows[1:]:
    # Get all cells in the row
    cells = row.find_all('td')
    # Check if there are enough cells
    if len(cells) >= 3:
        # Extract country name and population, stripping any
        leading/trailing white spaces
        # Also ensuring that we are only capturing the text
        and not any HTML tags or attributes
        country = cells[0].get_text(strip=True)
        population = cells[1].get_text(strip=True).
        replace(',', '')
        # Check if population data is numeric
        if population.isnumeric():
            # Add the country name and population to
            the data list
            data.append([country, population])

    # Return the populated data list
    return data

# Define a function to save the data to a CSV file
def save_to_csv(data, filename):
    # Open the file in write mode, ensuring UTF-8 encoding
    with open(filename, 'w', newline='', encoding='utf-8') as file:
```

```python
    # Create a CSV writer
    writer = csv.writer(file)
    # Write rows of data to the CSV file
    writer.writerows(data)

# Main execution starts here when the script is run directly
if __name__ == '__main__':
    # URL of the Wikipedia page containing the population data
    url = 'https://en.wikipedia.org/wiki/List_of_countries_and_
    dependencies_by_population'
    # Download the population data using the function defined above
    population_data = download_population_data(url)
    # Save the downloaded data to a CSV file using the function
defined above
    save_to_csv(population_data, 'Population.csv')
```

When you run the code, it will scrape the population data from the provided Wikipedia page and save it to a CSV file named "Population.csv" in the same directory as the Python script. The download_population_data function sends a GET request to a given URL, extracts the headers and rows from a table on the page, and stores the extracted data in a list. The save_to_csv function then writes this data to a CSV file. When the script is run directly, it fetches population data from a Wikipedia page and writes it to a CSV file.

To prepare for the Lesson 10 we need to generate sample data file. The following code accomplishes the goal by generating a random list of integers and None values for each column, then assembling those columns into a DataFrame, which is then written to a CSV file. None values in the DataFrame will be written as empty fields in the CSV. The use of random numbers means that the data will be different each time the code is run.

PYTHON CODE

```python
# Import pandas for data manipulation and random for generating
random numbers
import pandas as pd
import random

# Function to generate random data with some missing values
def generate_data():
    # Generate a list of 30 items where each item is either a
    random integer from 1 to 30 or None.
    # The choice between integer and None is made by generating
    another random number between 0 and 1,
    # and checking if it's greater than 0.2. If it is, we generate
    the random integer. If it's not,
    # we add None to the list. This means approximately 20% of the
    items in the list will be None,
    # representing missing values.
    return [random.randint(1, 30) if random.random() > 0.2 else
    None for _ in range(30)]
# Create a dictionary to hold our data. Each key is a string
representing the column name in the
```

```python
# resulting CSV, and the value is the list of data for that
# column, generated by our function above.
data = {
    'data1': generate_data(),
    'data2': generate_data(),
    'data3': generate_data(),
    'data4': generate_data(),
}


# Create a pandas DataFrame from our data. A DataFrame is a two-
# dimensional labeled data structure
# with columns potentially of different types. It's similar to a
# spreadsheet or SQL table, or a dict of
# Series objects.
df = pd.DataFrame(data)


# Write the DataFrame to a CSV file. index=False tells pandas not
# to write row numbers.
df.to_csv('data.csv', index=False)
```

LESSON 01.
MAZE SOLVER ON PAPER

Lesson Objectives:

The goal of this lesson is to introduce the concept of creating simple algorithms using the metaphor of maze-solving with robot commands. It's designed to instill in students the ability to formulate logical and conditional commands, effectively bolstering their problem-solving skills. This lesson will also guide students to reflect on the central role that planning and logical reasoning play in crafting effective algorithms. By the end of this lesson, students should be able to construct simple algorithms independently, demonstrating their understanding of the practical applications of algorithmic thinking.

Lesson Plan:

I.   Introduction to Maze Solver

   A. Overview of solving mazes using imaginary robot commands
   B. Understanding the available commands: Exit, If, Move, Wall, Turn, Repeat

II. Solving a Maze Step by Step

   A. Analyzing the maze and determining the starting point
   B. Following the path using the available commands
   C. Using conditionals (If) to make decisions based on walls or other conditions
   D. Navigating through the maze by moving, turning, and repeating actions
   E. Reaching the exit and determining if the maze is solved

III. Reflection and Discussion

   A. Discussing the process of solving the maze on paper
   B. Sharing different approaches and strategies used
   C. Reflecting on the importance of planning and logical thinking in maze-solving

Lesson Description:

This lesson introduces students to the concept of creating simple algorithms through the metaphor of maze-solving with robot commands. The initial phase familiarizes students with a variety of commands such as Exit, If, Move, Wall, Turn, Repeat, which are instrumental in formulating logical and conditional instructions.

The core part of the lesson unfolds as a step-by-step guide on using these commands to create an algorithm for solving a maze. Here, students learn to determine the starting point, create a pathway, and employ conditionals like 'If' to respond to different scenarios within the maze. This phase intensifies the students' understanding of executing movement, turning, and repeating actions, reinforcing their problem-solving skills.

As the lesson progresses, students are led to successfully create an algorithm that guides them to the maze's exit, hence solving the maze. The closing phase of the lesson encourages a reflection on the problem-solving process. It invites students to share their individual approaches and strategies, thereby promoting a collaborative learning experience. It underscores the importance of planning and logical reasoning in creating effective algorithms. By the end of the lesson, students are expected to construct simple algorithms independently, demonstrating their acquired skills in practical applications of algorithmic thinking.

Detailed Lesson Notes:

1.   Introduction to Maze Solver:

- Explain to the students that they will be solving a maze using imaginary robot commands, without any actual coding or technology.

- Introduce the available commands:
    - EXIT: Returns YES or NO to determine if the robot has reached the exit.
    - IF <CONDITION>: Allows the robot to perform actions based on certain conditions.
    - ELSE: Provides an alternative action if the condition in the IF statement is not met.
    - MOVE: Instructs the robot to move one step forward.
    - WALL (left|forward|right): Returns YES or NO to check if there is a wall on the left, forward, or right side of the robot.

- TURN (left|right): Instructs the robot to make a left or right turn.
- REPEAT <N TIMES>: Repeats a set of actions N times.
- REPEAT <SET OF ACTIONS> UNTIL <CONDITION>: Allows the robot to repeat a set of actions until a certain condition is met.

2. Solving a Maze Step by Step:

- Provide a maze diagram on paper for students to work on.

- Analyze the maze and determine the starting point.

- Follow the step-by-step approach to solve the maze, using the available commands.

- Example step-by-step process:
    1. Start at the designated starting point.
    2. Use conditionals (If) to check for walls or other conditions.
    3. Make decisions based on the conditions and take the appropriate actions (Move, Turn, Repeat).
    4. Repeat the actions until the exit is reached (Exit command).
    5. Determine if the maze is solved by checking the Exit command's response (YES or NO).

3. Reflection and Discussion:

-   Engage students in a discussion about their experience in solving the maze on paper.

-   Encourage them to share different approaches and strategies they used.

-   Discuss the importance of planning, logical thinking, and attention to detail in maze-solving.

-   Highlight the similarities between solving a maze on paper and writing code to solve mazes in programming.

Note:
It is essential to provide students with a visual maze diagram for them to follow along and apply the imaginary robot commands.

LESSON 02.
INTRODUCTION TO DATA, ALGORITHMS, AND PYTHON BASICS

Lesson Objectives:

The purpose of this lesson is to introduce students to the fundamental concepts of data and algorithms and their vital roles in programming. It aims to equip students with basic Python syntax, with a focus on variables, mathematical operations, and the use of print() and input() functions. Additionally, the lesson targets the creation and utilization of custom functions using def. With practical exercises, students will solidify their learning and be able to create simple Python programs. By the end of this lesson, students should be comfortable with Python's basic operations and be able to independently create a simple Python function.

Lesson Plan:

I.   Introduction to Data and Algorithms

    A. Definition and importance of data

    B. Overview of algorithms and their role in programming

    C. Relevance and application of data and algorithms in daily life

II. Python Basics

    A. Introduction to Python syntax

    B. Discussion on variables and the assignment operator (=)

    C. Basic math operations (+, -, *, /, **)

    D. The print() function and its usage

    E. The input() function and how to use it for interactive programs

    F. Creating and using functions with def

III. Practice Exercises

    A. Practical exercises on print() function, variables, and basic math operations

    B. Interactive exercise using input() function

    C. Creation of a simple multiplication function

IV. Summary and Homework

    A. Summary of the day's lesson

    B. Assign homework based on the lesson's content

    C. Answer any questions or doubts

Lesson Description:

The lesson initiates by imparting a fundamental understanding of data and algorithms, including their definitions, significance, and relevance in everyday life scenarios. The next segment of the lesson dives into Python basics, beginning with Python's syntax, before delving into concepts such as variables and the assignment operator. It then transitions into basic mathematical operations and the usage of print() and input() functions for creating interactive programs. The lesson also includes a detailed explanation of creating custom functions with 'def'.

The crux of the lesson is practical exercises aimed at reinforcing the understanding of print() function, variables, and basic math operations. It includes an interactive exercise utilizing the input() function and guides the students to create a simple multiplication function. The lesson concludes with a summary, followed by homework assignments that revolve around the content of the lesson. Lastly, there will be a Q&A segment to address any questions or doubts related to the lesson. The significant part of the lesson will be dedicated to hands-on exercises, which will help students apply their newly acquired knowledge.

Detailed Lesson Notes:

1. Start the lesson with an engaging discussion on the significance of data in today's digitally driven society. You could illustrate with examples like how Netflix recommends shows based on users' viewing habits (data), or how weather forecasts are made using historical and real-time climate data.

2. Transition into the concept of algorithms, describing them as a set of rules or instructions designed to perform specific tasks or solve particular problems.

Use everyday examples like a recipe for making pancakes or the steps in solving a mathematical problem.

3. Next, introduce Python programming language. Emphasize that Python is a versatile language, widely used in many fields including web development, data analysis, artificial intelligence, and more. Its simplicity and readability make it a great choice for beginners.

4. Introduce the concept of variables in Python. Explain that variables act as placeholders for data and the '=' symbol is used to assign a specific value to a variable. Demonstrate with the following code:

PYTHON CODE

```
x = 10   # Here, 'x' is a variable, and we're assigning the value '10' to it
y = "Python"   # 'y' is a variable, and we're assigning the string "Python" to it
```

---

5. Discuss the basic mathematical operations that Python can perform: addition (+), subtraction (-), multiplication (*), division (/), and exponentiation (**). Use the following code to illustrate:

PYTHON CODE

```python
a = 10
b = 2
print(a + b)    # Prints 12, because 10 + 2 = 12
print(a - b)    # Prints 8, because 10 - 2 = 8
print(a * b)    # Prints 20, because 10 * 2 = 20
print(a / b)    # Prints 5.0, because 10 / 2 = 5.0
print(a ** b)   # Prints 100, because 10 ** 2 = 100
                (10 raised to the power of 2)
```

PYTHON OUTPUT

```
12
8
20
5.0
100
```

6. Introduce the `print()` function. Explain that it's used to display information to the console. Show them how it works with different data types and the use of separator:

PYTHON CODE

```python
print("Hello, world!")   # Prints the string "Hello, world!"
print(5)   # Prints the integer 5
print("Hello", "world!", sep=', ')   # Prints "Hello, world!", with
words separated by a comma and a space
```

PYTHON OUTPUT

```
Hello, world!
5
Hello, world!
```

7. Discuss the `input()` function, which is used to get input from the user. Demonstrate with an example:

PYTHON CODE

```
name = input("Please enter your name: ")   # Asks the user to input their name
print("Hello, " + name)   # Greets the user with their name
```

PYTHON OUTPUT

```
Please enter your name: John
Hello, John
```

8. Explain the concept of functions in Python, highlighting that they are reusable pieces of code designed to perform a specific task. Show them how to define a function using `def` keyword:

PYTHON CODE

```python
def greet(name):   # Defines a function named 'greet' that takes one parameter 'name'
    print("Hello, " + name)   # The function prints a greeting that includes the name

greet("Alice")   # Calls the 'greet' function with the argument "Alice"
```

PYTHON OUTPUT

```
Hello, Alice
```

9. When going through exercises, ensure each student understands every line of code. For instance, when discussing `print('hello', 'world')`, explain that it prints the words "hello" and "world", separated by a space, to the console.

10. In the multiplication task, walk them through the process. Explain that Python interprets user input as a string, so they'll need to convert the input to an integer for multiplication. Here's an example:

PYTHON CODE

```python
num1 = int(input('Input the first number: '))   # Asks for the first number and converts it to an integer
```

```
num2 = int(input('Input the second number: '))  # Asks for the
second number and converts it to an integer
product = num1 * num2  # Multiplies the two numbers
print('The product is', product)  # Prints the product
```

PYTHON OUTPUT

```
Input the first number: 3
Input the second number: 4
The product is 12
```

---

11. Summarize the key points from the lesson, answering any lingering questions and clarifying doubts. Make sure students understand the fundamentals of Python introduced in this lesson: variables, basic operations, `print()`, `input()`, and functions.

12. For homework, ask them to create more Python functions, like a function that calculates and prints the area of a rectangle given its length and width. Or have them create a program that asks for a user's name and favorite color, then prints a personalized greeting.

LESSON 03.
BASIC PYTHON DATA TYPES, SYNTAX MISTAKES, TURTLE GRAPHICS AND LOOPS

Lesson Objectives:

This lesson intends to familiarize students with Python's essential data types such as str, int, float, and bool, through coding examples and exercises. It aims to expose students to common syntax errors in Python and methods to identify and rectify them. This lesson also plans to introduce students to the fun and engaging world of Turtle Graphics while teaching them the basics of Python loops using 'for' loops and the range() function. By incorporating creativity in coding, students will explore the synergy of Turtle Graphics and loops in creating complex and amusing shapes. By the end of this lesson, students should have an enriched understanding of Python's data types, error handling, loop structure, and be able to create visual masterpieces using Turtle Graphics.

Lesson Plan:

I.   Introduction to Python Data Types

A. Discussing str, int, float, and bool data types
B. Coding examples and exercises

II. Common Mistakes in Python

A. Exploration of typical syntax errors
B. Exercises in identifying and fixing these errors

III. Introduction to Turtle Graphics

A. Learning basic turtle commands
B. Creating shapes: circle and square
C. Manipulating the turtle: penup, pendown, clear
D. Changing pen color

IV. Understanding Python Loops

A. Explanation of 'for' loops and the range() function
B. Implementing loops in Turtle Graphics to draw a square and other shapes

V. Creative Coding with Turtle Graphics and Loops

A. Tasks involving changes to pen color, angle, and commands

B. Drawing a funny shape using loops and Turtle Graphics

VI. Recap and Q&A

A. Summarizing the day's lesson

B. Answering any questions or doubts

Lesson Description:

This lesson embarks with an exploration of the foundational data types in Python: strings (str), integers (int), floating-point numbers (float), and booleans (bool). To cultivate a practical understanding, students interact with coding examples and engage in exercises that demonstrate these fundamental data types.

Next, attention is drawn towards the common syntactical pitfalls that Python coders may stumble upon. By exposing students to these typical errors and guiding them through rectification exercises, this section aims to equip students with the acumen to avoid and resolve such errors independently.

Transitioning into a visually engaging segment, the lesson unveils the domain of Turtle Graphics. Students are shepherded through the usage of basic turtle commands, leading to the creation of elemental shapes. Beyond creation, learners are introduced to the manipulation of the turtle object through commands like penup, pendown, clear, and color changes.

As the lesson progresses, learners are familiarized with the 'for' loop construct in Python, along with the range() function. Leveraging these new tools, students apply loops within the Turtle Graphics environment to construct squares and more complex geometric figures. As a testament to creative freedom, learners then engage with assignments that inspire modifications to pen color, angular changes, and command alternations, fostering the creation of unique, visually intriguing shapes using loops and Turtle Graphics.

Rounding off the lesson is a comprehensive recapitulation of the day's learnings. This is complemented by a Q&A session, providing students an opportunity to resolve any queries, reinforce understandings, and stimulate curiosity about future lessons.

Detailed Lesson Notes:

1. Begin the lesson by discussing Python's basic data types and demonstrating them with code examples:

PYTHON CODE

```python
name = "Sandy"
print(name)
print(type(name))   # Output: <class 'str'>


age = 14
print(age)
print(type(age))   # Output: <class 'int'>


money = 9.99
print(money)
print(type(money))   # Output: <class 'float'>


done = True
print(done)
print(type(done))   # Output: <class 'bool'>
```

PYTHON OUTPUT

Sandy

```
<class 'str'>
14
<class 'int'>
9.99
<class 'float'>
True
<class 'bool'>
```

---

2. Discuss common mistakes in Python programming, demonstrating examples such as naming a variable starting with a number or using spaces in a variable name:

PYTHON CODE

```
# Incorrect variable naming
2nation = "hi"   # SyntaxError: invalid syntax
full name = "Ms Toms River"   # SyntaxError: invalid syntax
```

---

3. Transition into the use of Turtle Graphics. Import the turtle module and explain the basic commands for controlling the turtle. The ColabTurtle library is a Python module that was developed as a substitute for the turtle library in Google Colab notebooks. Here is how you can install and use it:

PYTHON CODE

```
!pip install ColabTurtle
# Import the ColabTurtle module. This module allows us to
create a "turtle" that we can move around the screen to draw
shapes and lines.
import ColabTurtle.Turtle as turtle

# Initialize turtle module
turtle.initializeTurtle()

# Change the shape of the turtle to look like a turtle. By
default, it's an arrow shape.
turtle.shape("turtle")

# Make the turtle move forward by 100 pixels. The turtle leaves a
trail behind it, effectively drawing a line.
turtle.forward(100)

# Rotate the turtle 90 degrees to the right. After this command,
any forward motion will be in this new direction.
turtle.right(90)

# Lift up the turtle's pen. After this command, the turtle can
move without drawing.
turtle.penup()

# Make the turtle move forward by 100 pixels. The turtle leaves a
trail behind it, effectively drawing a line.
turtle.forward(100)

# Put the turtle's pen down. After this command, the turtle will
resume drawing as it moves.
turtle.pendown()
```

```python
# Rotate the turtle 90 degrees to the right. After this command,
any forward motion will be in this new direction.
turtle.right(90)
# Make the turtle move forward by 100 pixels. The turtle leaves a
trail behind it, effectively drawing a line.
turtle.forward(100)
```

PYTHON OUTPUT

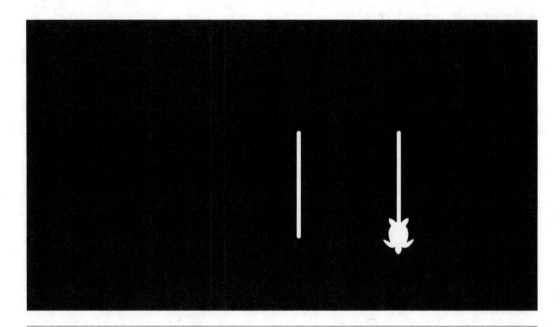

---

4. Introduce the concept of loops in Python, demonstrating the `for` loop and the `range()` function. The `for` loop in this code is a fundamental concept in computer programming, allowing you to repeat a block of code a specified number of times. This is particularly useful in drawing geometric shapes, where the same steps are often repeated multiple times.

PYTHON CODE

```python
for x in range(4):
    print(x)
```

PYTHON OUTPUT

```
0
1
2
3
```

5. Show students how to use Turtle Graphics to draw a square:

PYTHON CODE

```python
# Initialize turtle module
turtle.initializeTurtle()
# Change the shape of the turtle to look like a turtle. By
default, it's an arrow shape.
turtle.shape("turtle")

# Start a loop that will run 4 times. In Python, 'range(4)'
generates a sequence of numbers from 0 up to but not including 4.
for i in range(4):
    # Inside the loop, the turtle moves forward by 50 pixels.
    The turtle leaves a trail behind it, effectively
    drawing a line.
    turtle.forward(50)
```

```
# The turtle then turns 90 degrees to the right. After this
command, any subsequent forward motion will be in this
new direction.

turtle.right(90)

# End of loop. The loop will repeat the indented commands 4
times in total.
# This loop will cause the turtle to draw a square. Each
forward and right turn command forms one side of the square,
and the loop repeats this 4 times to form the complete square.
```

PYTHON OUTPUT

In this case, the use of the `for` loop is critical, allowing you to repeat the same instructions several times. In this example, the instructions are repeated 4

times, creating a square as the turtle moves forward and then turns right by 90 degrees in each iteration.

7. Show students how to create a funny shape using loops and Turtle Graphics. Discuss how changing the parameters affects the shape:

PYTHON CODE

```
# Initialize turtle module
turtle.initializeTurtle()
# Define a variable named 'angle' and set its value to 91. This
will be the angle by which the turtle will turn to the left in
each iteration of the loop.
angle = 91

# Show the turtle on the screen. Initially, the turtle is hidden,
so this command makes it visible.
turtle.showturtle()

# Change the shape of the turtle to look like a turtle. By
default, it's an arrow shape.
turtle.shape("turtle")

# Begin a loop that will run 100 times. 'range(100)' in
Python generates a sequence of numbers from 0 up to, but not
including, 100.
for x in range(100):
    # Inside the loop, the turtle draws a circle. The radius
    of the circle is equal to the current value of x, which
    increases with each iteration of the loop.
```

```
turtle.forward(x+50)

# The turtle then rotates to the left by the number of degrees
specified by 'angle' (91 degrees in this case).
turtle.left(angle)

# End of the loop. The loop will repeat the indented commands 100
times in total.

# This loop creates a spiral-like pattern of circles, with each
circle being larger than the previous one and rotated slightly
to the left.
```

PYTHON OUTPUT

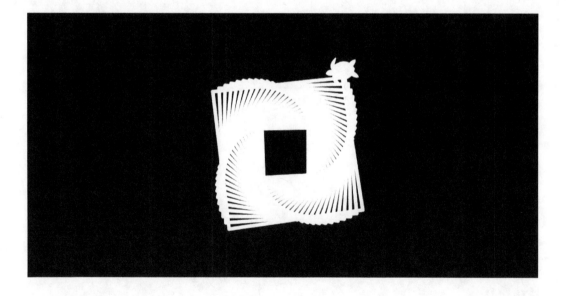

This code makes use of several concepts, including
variable assignment, loops, and using variables to modify
the behavior of functions dynamically. It results in an

interesting graphical pattern due to the gradual increase of the circle's size and the constant rotation.

8. For the tasks, ask students to:
    - Change the pen color to blue
    - Change the angle in the funny shape code to 33

9. Conclude the lesson by summarizing the key points and answering any questions students may have. Homework can include creating new designs with Turtle Graphics, experimenting with different Python data types, and identifying and fixing common Python errors.

LESSON 04.
CONDITIONAL STATEMENTS AND CONTROL FLOW

Lesson Objectives:

The purpose of this lesson is to expand students' proficiency in Python, focusing specifically on control flow structures. The lesson intends to revisit the foundational elements from earlier lessons—variables, basic mathematical operations, print(), input(), functions, and turtle graphics—and then advance to the pivotal concept of conditional statements. Through this lesson, students will explore comparison and logical operators, and learn to construct 'if', 'else', 'elif', 'while', and 'for' constructs. The ultimate aim is to enable students to manipulate the execution of their programs based on specific conditions and apply these techniques to resolve unique problem scenarios.

Lesson Plan:

I.   Recap and Warm-up

A. Briefly summarize the key points from the previous lessons.

B. Ask a few review questions to ensure students remember the basics of variables, basic math operations, `print()`, `input()`, and functions as well as turtle graphics.

II. Conditional Statements

A. Introduction to conditional statements and their role in decision-making.

B. Discuss the comparison operators (==, !=, <, >, <=, >=) and logical operators (and, or, not).

C. Demonstrate the `if` statement and explain its syntax.

D. Show examples of `if` statements with single and multiple conditions.

E. Introduce the `else` statement and explain its purpose.

F. Demonstrate the `if-else` statement and its syntax.

G. Provide examples of `if-else` statements.

III. Control Flow

A. Introduction to control flow and the concept of code execution based on conditions.

B. Explain the `elif` statement and its usage for multiple conditions.

C. Demonstrate nested `if` statements and discuss their structure.

D. Introduce the `while` loop and explain its syntax.

E. Show examples of `while` loops with conditionals.

F. Demonstrate the `for` loop and explain its syntax.

G. Provide examples of `for` loops.

IV. Practice Exercises

A. Practical exercises on conditional statements and control flow.

B. Write code snippets using `if`, `if-else`, `elif`, `while`, and `for` to solve specific problems.

C. Encourage students to think creatively and come up with their solutions.

V. Summary and Homework

A. Summarize the day's lesson, emphasizing the concepts of conditional statements and control flow.

B. Assign homework based on the lesson's content, including exercises that reinforce the use of conditional statements and control flow.

C. Answer any questions or doubts.

Lesson Description:

The lesson journey begins with a brief review of previous teachings, revitalizing students' knowledge of variables, basic math operations, the use of print() and input() functions, the creation of functions, and the utilization of turtle graphics.

Transitioning to the heart of the lesson—conditional statements—the lesson first establishes their crucial role in making programmatic decisions. Comparison operators (==, !=, <, >, <=, >=), which allow comparisons between values, and logical operators (and, or, not), which enable compound boolean expressions, are introduced. 'If' statements, a basic form of control flow that executes code based on whether a condition is true, are explored with illustrative examples.

The session then moves to 'else' statements, which offer alternative actions when the 'if' condition is not met. Students are presented with instances of 'if-else' constructions to understand their syntax and functionality. 'Elif', a contraction of 'else if', is also presented as a way to check multiple conditions and execute code accordingly.

Control flow, the order in which individual statements and functions are executed or evaluated, is the next topic of focus. Nested 'if' statements, where an 'if' or 'if-else' statement is contained within another, are analyzed to show how they can increase the flexibility and complexity of decision-making structures.

The lesson then dives into the 'while' loop that repeatedly executes code as long as a given condition is true, and the 'for' loop, which iterates over a sequence of values, often used with the range() function for a specified number of iterations.

Following the theoretical discussions, students are given a chance to apply their learning through practical exercises. They are tasked with employing 'if', 'if-else', 'elif', 'while', and 'for' statements in coding solutions for specific problem scenarios.

Finally, the lesson concludes with a summarization of the day's discoveries, putting particular emphasis on the understanding and application of control flow. Homework assignments, designed to further consolidate the lesson's learning, are provided. The session wraps up with an open forum for students to raise questions or clear any lingering confusion.

Detailed Lesson Notes:

1. Recap the previous lesson to refresh students' memory. Ask questions like:
   - What are variables, and how do you assign values to them in Python?
   - How do you perform basic math operations in Python?
   - What is the purpose of the `print()` function?
   - How do you get user input using the `input()` function?
   - What is a function, and how do you define and call one in Python?

2. Introduce conditional statements as structures that allow the program to make decisions based on certain conditions. Explain that conditions are created using comparison operators (==, !=, <, >, <=, >=) and logical operators (and, or, not).

3. Demonstrate the basic syntax of the `if` statement:

PYTHON CODE

```python
num = 7
if num % 2 == 0:
    print("The number is even.")
else:
    print("The number is odd.")
```

PYTHON OUTPUT

```
The number is odd.
```

---

6. Explain the concept of control flow, where the execution of code is influenced by conditions. Introduce the `elif` statement to check multiple conditions.

7. Demonstrate nested `if` statements, where an `if` statement is placed inside another `if` statement.

8. Show examples of `if` statements with single and multiple conditions:

PYTHON CODE

```python
age = 25
if age >= 18:
    print("You are an adult.")


temperature = 25
if temperature > 30:
    print("It's hot!")
elif temperature < 10:
    print("It's cold!")
else:
    print("The weather is moderate.")
```

PYTHON OUTPUT

```
You are an adult.
The weather is moderate.
```

9. Introduce the `while` loop, which repeats a block of code as long as a condition is True. Explain its syntax:

PYTHON CODE

```python
while condition:  # Code block to execute repeatedly
```

10. Show examples of `while` loops with conditionals:

PYTHON CODE

```python
count = 1
while count <= 5:
    print("Count:", count)
    count += 1
```

PYTHON OUTPUT

```
Count: 1
Count: 2
Count: 3
Count: 4
Count: 5
```

11. Explain the `for` loop, which iterates over a sequence of elements, one more time. Discuss its syntax:

PYTHON CODE

```python
for variable in sequence:
    # Code block to execute for each iteration
```

12. Provide examples of `for` loops:

PYTHON CODE

```python
fruits = ["apple", "banana", "cherry"]
for fruit in fruits:
        print("Fruit:", fruit)
```

PYTHON OUTPUT

```
Fruit: apple
Fruit: banana
Fruit: cherry
```

---

13. During the practice exercises, encourage students to analyze the problem and come up with their solutions using conditional statements and control flow. For example, ask them to write code that checks if a given number is prime or to create a program that prints the multiplication table of a given number.

14. Summarize the key points covered in the lesson, ensuring that students understand the concepts of conditional statements, comparison operators, logical operators, control flow, `if` statements, `else` statements, `if-else` statements, `elif` statements, `while` loops, and `for` loops.

15. Assign homework that includes exercises related to conditional statements and control flow. For example, ask students to write a program that determines if a year is a leap year or not. Another task could be to create a program that counts the occurrences of each character in a given string.

LESSON 05.
EXPANDING ON TURTLE GRAPHICS AND INTRODUCTION TO PYTHON FUNCTIONS

Lesson Objectives:

The purpose of this session is to delve deeper into the Python programming language, focusing on the concept of functions and their applications. Students will learn about the `def` command, the principle of parameters and return values, and how functions facilitate code reuse and simplification. Furthermore, the lesson aims to provide an interactive learning experience where students will implement an arrow game using functions, applying their newly acquired skills. By the end of the session, students should be able to articulate the principles of

Python functions, create their own functions, and utilize them in the context of a simple game.

Lesson Plan:

I.   Recap of Basic Turtle Commands

   A. Quick review of basic Turtle commands
   B. Encouraging students to share their experiences with using the Turtle library so far

II. Introduction to Python Functions

   A. Explanation of the `def` command and how it's used to create functions in Python
   B. Exploring the concept of parameters and return values
   C. Demonstrating how to use functions to simplify and reuse code

III. Creating an Interactive Arrow Game

   A. Explanation and demonstration of the `onclick()` function for user interaction
   B. Discussion on the use of Python functions to create a simple interactive arrow game

C. Coding exercise: Building the arrow game with functions

IV. Review and Q&A

A. Reviewing the day's lesson
B. Time for questions and answers

Lesson Description:

The educational journey kicks off with a swift recap of the rudimentary commands associated with Python's Turtle library. To make the revision session more interactive and collaborative, students are encouraged to share their experiences with the Turtle library, recounting their successes and challenges.

Transitioning into the core of the lesson, the spotlight is cast on Python's functions, focusing on the use of the `def` command. This portion of the lesson elucidates how `def` is employed to establish functions within Python, and explores the concepts of parameters and return values. With the goal of demonstrating the practical implications of functions, students are shown how these structures can be utilized to simplify their code and promote reusability, enhancing the efficiency of their programming practices.

Proceeding further, students are introduced to the `onclick()` function, a crucial tool in facilitating user interaction within their Python projects. The objective of this segment is to enable students to understand and implement this function, culminating in a hands-on exercise where they employ functions to construct an interactive arrow game. This dynamic exercise not only solidifies their understanding of Python functions but also underscores the practical applications of these concepts in creating interactive Python projects.

Concluding the session is a comprehensive review of the day's learnings, accompanied by a Q&A segment. This allows the students to clear any uncertainties, consolidate their understanding, and engage in a thoughtful discussion about the concepts explored throughout the lesson.

Important Note:

This lesson makes use of the `turtle` library in Python which supports GUI and interactive programming. Unfortunately, these features are not supported in the Google Colab environment due to its limited graphical display capabilities. In Google Colab, the graphical display is mainly restricted to static images, charts, and tables generated with libraries such as Matplotlib or Seaborn. Even the adapted version of the library for Colab, `ColabTurtle`, does not support the full feature set of the standard `turtle` library.

Therefore, to fully engage with this lesson, I recommend using an environment that supports the full `turtle` library and its interactive capabilities. One such environment is [Repl.it](https://repl.it/). Repl.it is an online coding platform that supports Python and many other languages. It also supports graphical output, which makes it a great choice for this lesson.

To use Repl.it:

1. Navigate to [Repl.it](https://repl.it/).

2. Sign up for a free account or log in if you already have one.

3. Click on the "+ new repl" button to create a new repl.

4. Select Python as the language.

5. Paste the code from this lesson into the code editor and click 'Run'.

You should now be able to fully interact with this lesson, clicking on the graphics window to move the 'arrow' turtle, and observing the results as you attempt to hit the 'target' turtle.

Detailed Lesson Notes:

1. Start by reviewing the basic Turtle library commands. Encourage students to share their experiences, challenges, and achievements using the library so far.

2. Refresh the concept of Python functions. Explain that functions are reusable pieces of code that can perform a task. They can accept inputs, known as parameters, and produce output, known as a return value. Here's a simple example of a Python function:

PYTHON CODE

```python
def say_hello():    # Defines a function named 'say_hello'
    print("Hello!")   # The function prints "Hello!"
say_hello()   # Calls the 'say_hello' function
```

PYTHON OUTPUT

```
Hello!
```

---

3. Discuss parameters and return values in depth. Explain that parameters are the variables listed inside the parentheses in the function definition, and the return value is the result that the function produces. Demonstrate this with a function that calculates the sum of two numbers:

PYTHON CODE

```python
def add_numbers(num1, num2):   # Defines a function 'add_numbers'
that takes two parameters: 'num1' and 'num2'
    return num1 + num2   # The function adds the two parameters
and returns the result
result = add_numbers(5, 3)   # Calls the 'add_numbers' function
with arguments 5 and 3
print(result)   # Prints the result
```

PYTHON OUTPUT

8

---

4. Introduce the `onclick()` function in the Turtle library. Explain that it's used to capture user mouse clicks on the Turtle screen. The function takes two parameters: a function to be executed when a click occurs and the number of the mouse button that will

trigger the function (1 for the left button, 2 for the middle button, 3 for the right button).

5. Transition into the interactive arrow game. Start by defining the initial setup of the game, including the target and arrow:

PYTHON CODE

```python
import turtle
import random

# Create a new turtle screen and set its background color
screen = turtle.Screen()
screen.bgcolor("skyblue")

# Create a target turtle
target = turtle.Turtle()
target.shape("circle")
target.color("red")
target.penup()
target.goto(random.randint(-100, 100), random.randint(-100, 100))

# Create an arrow turtle
arrow = turtle.Turtle()
arrow.color("black")
arrow.penup()
```

---

6. Define the function that will be executed when the user clicks the screen. This function should move the arrow towards the click's location and then check if it hit the target:

PYTHON CODE

```
def move_arrow(x, y):
    arrow.goto(x, y)   # Move the arrow to the click's location
    if arrow.distance(target) < 15:   # If the arrow is close to
the target (less than 15 units)
            print("Hit!")   # Print "Hit!"
            target.goto(random.randint(-100, 100),
            random.randint(-100, 100))   # Move the target to a new
random location
        else:
            print("Miss!")   # Print "Miss!"

    # Bind the 'move_arrow' function to mouse clicks
screen.onclick(move_arrow, 1)
```

---

7. Summarize the key concepts of the lesson, allowing time for students to ask questions and clarifying any doubts they may have. For homework, students could be tasked to expand the game by adding multiple targets, creating a scoring system, or incorporating other ideas they might have.

8. Start the Turtle graphics loop. This is needed for mouse clicks to be captured and to keep the Turtle graphics window open:

PYTHON CODE

```
turtle.mainloop()
```

PYTHON OUTPUT

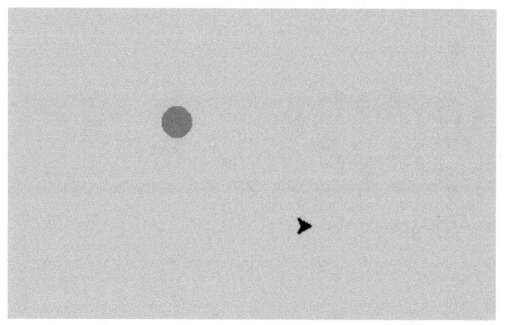

Hit!

LESSON 06.
UNDERSTANDING WHILE LOOPS, RANDOM NUMBERS, HCF, AND PRIME NUMBERS IN PYTHON

Lesson Objectives:

This lesson aims to strengthen students' understanding of core programming concepts in Python, such as While loops, random number generation, the modulo operator, and the Highest Common Factor (HCF). Additionally, it seeks to introduce the concept of prime numbers and their detection using Python functions. By the conclusion of the lesson, students should be capable of implementing While loops, generating random numbers, calculating the HCF, and distinguishing prime numbers within a given range, thereby broadening their programming skills and mathematical knowledge.

Lesson Plan:

I.   Understanding While Loops and Random Numbers

A. Discussing the concept and usage of While loops in Python

B. Discussing what random numbers are and how to generate them in Python

C. Running a While loop to generate random numbers

II.   Introduction to Modulo Operator and the Highest Common Factor (HCF)

A. Introducing the modulo operator in Python

B. Explaining the concept of HCF and its relevance

C. Finding the HCF of two numbers using recursion

D. Finding the HCF of two numbers using a While loop

III. Understanding Prime Numbers and Implementing Prime Number Check

A. Defining prime numbers and their significance

B. Creating a function to check if a number is prime

C. Using the function to find all prime numbers within a range

IV. Review and Q&A

A. Summarizing the key points of the lesson
B. Opening the floor for questions and answers

Lesson Description:

Kicking off the lesson, the focus initially falls on Python's While loops. Students will be introduced to the concept and application of While loops in Python, explaining how they facilitate iterative tasks. The lesson then shifts towards the generation of random numbers, utilizing Python's `random` library to illustrate this.

Next, the modulo operator is spotlighted, providing an explanation of its functionality and its essential role in programming and mathematical computations. With a focus on concrete applications, the concept of the Highest Common Factor (HCF) is presented, illustrating its importance in number theory and its utility in various calculations. Students are then guided through finding the HCF of two numbers using two different methods—firstly, by using recursion, a programming technique involving a function that calls itself, and secondly, by using a While loop, reinforcing their practical understanding of the concept.

The lesson then introduces the mathematical concept of prime numbers, establishing their definition and their relevance. Using this foundational knowledge, students are guided through creating a function to determine whether a number is prime. This function is then used to identify all prime numbers within a given range, demonstrating a practical application of the function and reinforcing the learning objective.

The lesson wraps up with a summary of the key concepts discussed throughout the session. A question and answer session follows the summary, providing students with the opportunity to clarify any uncertainties and consolidate their understanding of the lesson's key points.

Detailed Lesson Notes:

1. Start the lesson by introducing the concept of While loops in Python. While loops are a type of control flow statement that allows code to be executed repeatedly based on a given Boolean condition.

2. Explain what random numbers are. In the context of programming, random numbers are numbers that a computer generates where the next number in the sequence can't be predicted. This is useful for many kinds of programming tasks, such as generating unique ids, simulations, and games.

3. Demonstrate how to use Python's built-in library function randint() to generate random numbers. Using a While loop, generate random numbers until it produces a number larger than 20.

PYTHON CODE

```python
import random as rnd
a_number = 0
while a_number <= 20:
    a_number = rnd.randint(1, 25)
    print("This is the random number:", a_number)
print("You have found one larger than 20")
```

PYTHON OUTPUT

```
This is the random number: 13
This is the random number: 8
This is the random number: 3
This is the random number: 17
This is the random number: 19
This is the random number: 1
This is the random number: 23
You have found one larger than 20
```

---

4. Introduce the modulo operator (%). This operator gives the remainder of a division operation. For example, 10 % 3 will result in 1 because when 10 is divided by 3, the remainder is 1. Introduce the floor division operator (//), which performs division and rounds down to the nearest whole number, for example, 10 // 3 equals 3 because it divides 10 by 3 and returns the quotient rounded down to the nearest integer.

5. Explain the concept of HCF (Highest Common Factor). The HCF of two integers is the largest integer that evenly divides (without a remainder) each of the two numbers.

6. Demonstrate how to calculate the HCF, check for possible errors in the user input and double check the results:

PYTHON CODE

```
# Function to calculate the Highest Common Factor (HCF) using the
Euclidean Algorithm
def hcf(a, b):
  if(b == 0):
    return abs(a)
  else:
    return hcf(b, a % b)

# Prompt the user to enter the first number
x = input("Enter the first number: ")

# Prompt the user to enter the second number
```

```python
y = input("Enter the second number: ")

# Try-except block to handle any input errors
try:
    # Convert the inputs to integers
    a = int(x)
    b = int(y)
# If inputs can't be converted to integers, print an error message
except ValueError:
    print("Both inputs must be integers.")
# If no errors were encountered in the try block, proceed
else:
    # Compute and display the HCF using the defined function
    print(f"The HCF of {a} and {b} is: ", end="")
    output = hcf(a, b)
    print(output)

    # Double-checking the result
    # Initialize the maximum HCF to 1
    max_hcf = 1
    # Iterate through all integers up to the minimum of a and b
    for i in range(1, min(a, b) + 1):
        # If a and b are both divisible by i, update max_hcf
        if a % i == b % i == 0:
        max_hcf = i
    # Compare the calculated HCF with the double checked HCF
    if max_hcf == output:
        print("Double check passed: The HCF is correct.")
    else:
        print(f"Double check failed: Expected {max_hcf},
        but got {output}.")
```

PYTHON OUTPUT

Enter the first number: 28
Enter the second number: 64
The HCF of 28 and 64 is: 4
Double check passed: The HCF is correct.

---

7. Show students another way to calculate the HCF, this time using a While loop and the modulo operator:

PYTHON CODE

```python
# Ask for the first number from the user
x = input("Enter the first number: ")

# Ask for the second number from the user
y = input("Enter the second number: ")

# To handle any input errors
try:
    # Convert the inputs to integers
    a = int(x)
    b = int(y)
# If the inputs cannot be converted to integers, an error
message is printed
except ValueError:
    print("Both inputs must be integers.")
# If there are no errors in the 'try' block, then the 'else'
block executes
```

```
else:
    # Start of Euclidean Algorithm: keep running while
    b is not zero
    while b != 0:
        # In each loop iteration, replace a with b and b
        with the remainder of a / b
        a, b = b, a % b

    # After the loop ends, a is the highest common factor
    (HCF) of the original a and b
    print("The HCF is: ", a)
```

PYTHON OUTPUT

```
Enter the first number: 28
Enter the second number: 64
The HCF is:   4
```

---

8. Transition into the topic of prime numbers. A prime number is a natural number greater than 1 that has no positive divisors other than 1 and itself. For example, 2, 3, 5, 7, 11, 13, 17, and 19 are all prime numbers.

9. Show students how to create a function that checks if a number is prime by trying to divide it by all numbers up to its square root. If any division results in a whole number, the original number is not prime.

PYTHON CODE

```python
# Define a function to check if a number is prime
def isPrime(n):
    # If the number is 0 or 1, it's not prime
    if(n==1 or n==0):
        return False
    # For all numbers from 2 to n
    for i in range(2, n):
        # If n is divisible by any number other than
        1 and itself, it's not prime
        if(n%i==0):
            return False
    # If none of the above conditions are met,
    the number is prime
    return True
```

10. Lastly, use the `isPrime` function to find all the prime numbers within a user-input range:

PYTHON CODE

```python
# Try to get a number from the user
try:
    # Ask the user for a number
    N = int(input("Input number: "))
# If the user's input isn't a number, print an error message
except ValueError:
    print("Input must be an integer.")
# If the user's input is a number, proceed with the else block
```

```
else:
        # Loop through all numbers from 1 to N
        for i in range(1, N+1):
                # If the number is prime, print it
                if(isPrime(i)):
                        print(i, end=" ")
```

PYTHON OUTPUT

Input number: 34
2 3 5 7 11 13 17 19 23 29 31

11. Review the key points from the lesson, and invite any questions the students may have. Students can practice their new skills by trying to solve problems that involve the modulo operator, HCF, prime numbers, and While loops.

LESSON 07.
EXPLORING LISTS, STRINGS, AND STRING MANIPULATION IN PYTHON

Lesson Objectives:

The intent of this lesson is to delve deeper into Python's data structures, specifically strings and lists. Students will learn about the characteristics and utilities of these structures and master the skills of string indexing, slicing, and list operations. Furthermore, they will develop their problem-solving abilities by addressing practical tasks like removing consecutive duplicates from a string and splitting a number into its digits. By the end of this session, students should be able to manipulate Python strings and lists comfortably and demonstrate their knowledge by tackling problems that require a good understanding of these data structures.

Lesson Plan:

I. Introduction to Strings and Indexing

A. Explaining the concept of strings in Python

B. Understanding string indexing and how to access individual characters

C. Practicing string slicing to extract specific parts of a string

II. Understanding Lists and List Operations

A. Introduction to Python lists and their utility

B. Creation of lists with various types of values (numbers, strings, mixed)

C. Explanation of multi-dimensional lists

D. Accessing elements from a list, including multi-dimensional lists

III. String Manipulation: Removing Duplicates

A. Discussing a problem statement: removing consecutive duplicates from a string

B. Creating a function to solve the problem

C. Testing the function with a string

IV. Number Splitting and List Manipulation

A. Discussing another problem: splitting a number into its digits and storing them in a list
B. Creating a function to solve the problem
C. Testing the function with a number

V. Practical Application: Working with Random Numbers in a List

A. Task description: creating a list of 10 random numbers, printing the list, and finding the minimum and maximum numbers
B. Students will code along to complete the task
C. Discussing the output and any challenges faced

VI. Review and Q&A

A. Summarizing the key points of the lesson
B. Opening the floor for questions and answers

Lesson Description:

The lesson initiates by introducing students to Python strings, an immutable sequence of Unicode characters. The idea of string indexing is covered next, highlighting how to access individual characters in a string using their index. Students then get hands-on experience with string slicing, a technique that extracts a portion of a string based on index positions.

Shifting the focus onto Python lists, the second part of the lesson discusses the versatility of lists as they can contain elements of various types, like numbers, strings, and even other lists. To ensure an in-depth understanding, students create lists with different types of values. A more advanced concept of multi-dimensional lists is also introduced, alongside how to access elements from them.

In the third segment, the lesson dives into a real-world problem of removing consecutive duplicates from a string. Students engage in the process of creating a Python function to address this issue, consequently testing it to ensure its effectiveness. This segment serves to further cement the understanding of strings and introduces the practical aspect of problem-solving.

The next part deals with another common problem — splitting a number into its digits and storing them in a list. Again, students are tasked with creating a function to solve this, thus solidifying their understanding of Python's handling of numbers and lists.

In the penultimate segment, students tackle a practical task that involves generating a list of random numbers, using Python's `random` library, and determining the minimum and maximum numbers in that list. This session affords students the opportunity to apply their knowledge in a practical scenario, also opening up discussions on the output and challenges encountered.

Finally, the lesson concludes with a review of the day's topics and a Q&A session, allowing students to clarify any doubts or questions they might have about the content, further solidifying their grasp of Python's strings and lists.

Detailed Lesson Notes:

1. Begin the lesson by introducing the concept of strings in Python. A string is a sequence of characters. In Python, string literals are enclosed in either single quotes (' ') or double quotes (" ").

2. Explain how to access characters in a string using indexing. In Python, indexing syntax can be used as a substitute for the substring function. This is an effortless way of extracting a part of a string.

PYTHON CODE

```python
String1 = "Machine Learning For Kids"
print("\nFirst character of String is: ")
print(String1[0])
print("\nLast character of String is: ")
print(String1[-1])
```

PYTHON OUTPUT

```
First character of String is:
M

Last character of String is:
s
```

3. Introduce the concept of string slicing. This feature enables us to extract and introduce a segment of a string (substring).

PYTHON CODE

```python
print("\nSlicing characters from 3-12: ")
print(String1[3:12])
```

PYTHON OUTPUT

```
Slicing characters from 3-12:
hine Lear
```

4. Transition into the concept of lists in Python. Lists are one of the most powerful tools in Python. They are used to store an ordered collection of items, which might be of different types but usually they aren't. Commas separate the elements that are contained within a list and enclosed in square brackets.

5. Show students how to create lists with different types of values and how to access elements from a list.

PYTHON CODE

```
List = [10, 20, 14]
List = ["Machine", "Learning", "For", "Kids"]
List = [1, 2, 'Machine', 4,'Learning', 6, 'Python']
```

6. Introduce the concept of multi-dimensional lists. A Multi-Dimensional list means a list within a list. In Python, the list can contain different types of elements like integers, strings, lists, etc.

7. Discuss the problem of removing consecutive duplicates from a string and guide students through creating a function to solve this problem. The removeDuplicates function goes through each character in the string and compares it with the previous character. If they're different, it adds the character to a list. The function then joins the list into a string, effectively removing any consecutive duplicates.

PYTHON CODE

```python
# Define a function to remove consecutive duplicates from a string
def removeDuplicates(s):
    # Initialize an empty list to store the unique characters
    chars = []
    # Initialize a variable to keep track of the
    previous character
    prev = None
    # For each character in the input string
    for c in s:
        # If the current character is different from
        the previous one
        if prev != c:
            # Add the current character to the list
            chars.append(c)
            # Update the previous character
            prev = c
    # Join the characters in the list into a string
    and return it
    return ''.join(chars)
```

```python
# Ask the user to input a string
s = input("Enter a string: ")

# Apply the function to the user's string and store the result
output = removeDuplicates(s)

# Print the resulting string
print("The string without consecutive duplicates is: ", output)
```

PYTHON OUTPUT

```
Enter a string: HHaaMmhei3
The string without consecutive duplicates is: HaMmhei3
```

8. Discuss another problem: splitting a number into its digits and storing them in a list. Show students how to solve this problem using recursion and list manipulation. The split_number function uses recursion to divide the number by 10 repeatedly, adding the remainder at each step to a list. This effectively splits the number into its individual digits.

PYTHON CODE

```python
# Define a recursive function to split a number into its digits
def split_number(num, result):
    # If the number is greater than 0
    if num > 0:
```

```python
        # Call the function on the number divided
        by 10 (integer division)
        split_number(num // 10, result)
        # Add the remainder when the number is divided
        by 10 to the result list
        result.append(num % 10)


# Ask the user to input a number
num = input("Enter a number: ")


# Try to convert the user's input to an integer
try:
        num = int(num)
# If the conversion fails, print an error message
except ValueError:
        print("Input must be an integer.")
# If the conversion succeeds, proceed with the else block
else:
        # Initialize an empty list to store the digits
        result = []
        # Call the function on the user's number
        split_number(num, result)
        # Print the resulting list of digits
        print("The split number is: ", result)
```

PYTHON OUTPUT

Enter a number: 2345625736869
The split number is: [2, 3, 4, 5, 6, 2, 5, 7, 3, 6, 8, 6, 9]

9. For the final exercise, guide students through creating a list of 10 random numbers, printing the list, and finding the minimum and maximum numbers. This practical application will help consolidate their understanding of lists and string operations.

10. Summarize the key points of the lesson and invite any questions from the students.

LESSON 08.
TULIPS, DICTIONARIES
AND RECURSION

Lesson Objectives:

The focal point of this lesson is to introduce students to the core Python data structures, namely tuples and dictionaries, and the concept of recursion. It aims to demonstrate the significance of these data structures in organizing and managing data in programming, along with the benefits of recursion for solving intricate problems. By the end of this session, students should be able to create, manipulate and utilize tuples and dictionaries effectively, and understand the implementation of recursive functions.

Lesson Plan:

I. Introduction to Python Data Structures

A. Discussing the importance of data organization and storage in programming

B. Introducing Python data structures: Tuples, Dictionaries and their properties

C. Illustrating how data structures can be used to solve real-world problems

II. Delving into Tuples

A. Explaining the concept of Tuples and their characteristics

B. Demonstrating the creation of Tuples using Python syntax

C. Discussing common Tuple operations: Indexing, Slicing, and Concatenation

D. Explaining when to use Tuples over other data structures

III. Understanding Dictionaries

A. Discussing the significance of Dictionaries and their uses

B. Demonstrating how to create and access elements from a Dictionary

C. Highlighting common Dictionary methods like `keys()`, `values()`, and `items()`

D. Explaining how to modify and delete key-value pairs from a Dictionary

IV. Unveiling Recursion

A. Defining recursion and its importance in programming

B. Illustrating the mechanism of a recursive function using an example

C. Demonstrating how recursion can be used to solve complex problems with simple and elegant solutions

D. Comparing iterative and recursive approaches to problem-solving

V. Review and Q&A

A. Summarizing the key concepts covered in the lesson, including Tuples, Dictionaries, and Recursion

B. Addressing any questions or concerns from the students

C. Encouraging further exploration of Python through additional resources and practice exercises

Lesson Description:

The lesson starts off by underscoring the importance of data organization and storage in programming. Here, the spotlight is on Python's data structures: tuples and dictionaries. Students will understand the role these structures play in solving real-world problems, setting the stage for more in-depth exploration of these concepts.

Delving into tuples, the lesson outlines the characteristics of tuples – they are ordered, immutable collections. Students will witness how to create tuples using Python syntax and carry out common tuple operations such as indexing, slicing, and concatenation. The students will also gain an understanding of when to employ tuples over other data structures, providing them with a strategic advantage in decision making during programming.

Subsequently, dictionaries, Python's mutable and dynamic data structures that store key-value pairs, are introduced. Students will learn how to create a dictionary and access its elements, besides getting acquainted with dictionary methods such as `keys()`, `values()`, and `items()`. Also, the lesson covers how to modify and delete key-value pairs from a dictionary, essential skills for handling this data structure.

In the fourth segment, the lesson unearths the concept of recursion, a method where the solution to a problem depends on solutions to smaller instances of the same problem. Through examples, students will unravel the mechanism of a recursive function, and see how recursion can offer simple and elegant solutions to complex problems. The lesson also highlights the comparison between iterative and recursive approaches, broadening students' problem-solving toolbox.

To conclude, the lesson wraps up with a comprehensive review of the covered concepts – tuples, dictionaries, and recursion. A dedicated Q&A session provides students the opportunity to clarify doubts and gain a deeper understanding of these Python constructs. Lastly, students are encouraged to continue exploring Python through additional resources and practice exercises, reinforcing a culture of independent learning.

Detailed Lesson Notes:

I. Introduction to Python Data Structures

- Discuss the importance of data organization and storage in programming, emphasizing the necessity for different data structures to accommodate different data handling needs.
- Introduce Python data structures: Tuples, Dictionaries. Mention their properties and usage scenarios.

II. Delving into Tuples

- Explain the concept of a Tuple and its characteristics. A Tuple is an ordered collection of Python objects, and unlike lists, they are immutable.

PYTHON CODE

```python
# There is no need for a specific import statement to use
Tuples in Python
tuple_example = (1, 'a', True)  # A Tuple containing different
types of data
print(tuple_example)  # Output: (1, 'a', True)
```

PYTHON OUTPUT

```
(1, 'a', True)
```

- Discuss common Tuple operations such as:
    - Indexing: Access an item in a tuple using its index.

PYTHON CODE

```python
print(tuple_example[0])  # Output: 1
```

PYTHON OUTPUT

```
1
```

    - Slicing: Get a range of items from a tuple.

PYTHON CODE

```python
print(tuple_example[:2])  # Output: (1, 'a')
```

PYTHON OUTPUT

```
(1, 'a')
```

    - Concatenation: Combine two tuples into a new one.

PYTHON CODE

```python
tuple_example2 = ('hello', 2.5)
print(tuple_example + tuple_example2)  # Output: (1, 'a', True, 'hello', 2.5)
```

(1, 'a', True, 'hello', 2.5)

- Explain when to use Tuples over other data structures.

III. Understanding Dictionaries

- Discuss the significance of Dictionaries.

PYTHON CODE

```
dictionary_example = {'name': 'Alice', 'age': 12, 'school': 'Middle
School'}   # A Dictionary with key-value pairs
print(dictionary_example)   # Output: {'name': 'Alice', 'age': 12,
'school': 'Middle School'}
```

PYTHON OUTPUT

{'name': 'Alice', 'age': 12, 'school': 'Middle School'}

- Demonstrate how to create and access elements from a Dictionary.

PYTHON CODE

```python
print(dictionary_example['name'])  # Output: Alice
```

PYTHON OUTPUT

```
Alice
```

- Highlight common Dictionary methods:
    - `keys()` – returns a view object that displays a list of all the keys.

PYTHON CODE

```python
print(dictionary_example.keys())  # Output: dict_keys(['name', 'age', 'school'])
```

PYTHON OUTPUT

```
dict_keys(['name', 'age', 'school'])
```

- `values()` – returns a view object that displays a list of all the values.

PYTHON CODE

```python
print(dictionary_example.values())  # Output: dict_values(['Alice', 12, 'Middle School'])
```

PYTHON OUTPUT

dict_values(['Alice', 12, 'Middle School'])

- `items()` – returns a view object that displays a list of dictionary's (key, value) tuple pairs.

PYTHON CODE

```python
print(dictionary_example.items())  # Output: dict_items([('name', 'Alice'), ('age', 12), ('school', 'Middle School')])
```

PYTHON OUTPUT

```
dict_items([('name', 'Alice'), ('age', 12), ('school', 'Middle School')])
```

- Explain how to modify and delete key-value pairs from a Dictionary.

PYTHON CODE

```python
dictionary_example['age'] = 13  # Modify value
del dictionary_example['school']  # Delete key-value pair
```

IV. Unveiling Recursion

- Define recursion.

- Illustrate the mechanism of a recursive function using an example.

PYTHON CODE

```python
def factorial(n):
    """Returns the factorial of a number."""
    if n == 1:
        return 1
    else:
        return n * factorial(n-1)

print("Factorial of 5 is:",factorial(5))
```

PYTHON OUTPUT

Factorial of 5 is: 120

- Demonstrate how recursion can be used to solve complex problems with simple and elegant solutions.

PYTHON CODE

```python
def fibonacci(n):
    """Returns the nth Fibonacci number."""
    if n <= 1:
```

```
        return n
    else:
        return (fibonacci(n-1) + fibonacci(n-2))


print("15th Fibonacci number is:", fibonacci(15))
```

PYTHON OUTPUT

```
15th Fibonacci number is: 610
```

- Compare iterative and recursive approaches to problem-solving.

V.   Review and Q&A

- Summarize the key concepts covered in the lesson.

- Address any questions or concerns from the students.

- Encourage students to explore Python further through additional resources and practice exercises.

LESSON 09.
INTRODUCTION TO MACHINE LEARNING AND DATA VISUALIZATION IN PYTHON

Lesson Objectives:

The objective of this lesson is to introduce students to the basics of machine learning, data visualization using Python, and handling data stored in CSV files. The students will have a hands-on experience with Teachable Machines Image Experiments, learn how to visualize data using bar charts, and apply this knowledge to CSV data. By the end of this session, students will gain an appreciation for machine learning, be comfortable with visualizing data, and understand the fundamental aspects of CSV file operations in Python.

Lesson Plan:

I. Introduction to Machine Learning

A. Explain the concept of machine learning

B. Differentiate between supervised and unsupervised learning

II. Hands-on Activity: Teachable Machines Image Experiments

A. Demonstrate the "Rock, Paper, Scissors" and "Cats vs Dogs" image experiments using Teachable Machines

III. Introduction to Data Visualization with Python

A. Explain the importance of data visualization

B. Demonstrate how to create a bar chart using a list of values

IV. Reading Data from CSV Files

A. Introduce CSV (Comma Separated Values) files and their utility in data storage

B. Show how to read data from a CSV file using Python's built-in `open` function

C. Introduce the `with open` statement for efficient file handling

V. Practical Application: Creating a Bar Chart from CSV Data

  A. Task description: Create a bar chart depicting the number of medals won by different teams, with data sourced from a CSV file

  B. Students will code along to complete the task

  C. Discussing the output and any challenges faced

VI. Review and Q&A

  A. Summarizing the key points of the lesson

  B. Opening the floor for questions and answers

Lesson Description:

The lesson kicks off with an introduction to machine learning, an application of artificial intelligence (AI) that provides systems the ability to automatically learn and improve from experience without being explicitly programmed. Students will learn about the two main types of machine learning: supervised learning, where the machine learns from labeled data, and unsupervised learning, where the machine discovers hidden patterns in unlabeled data.

The second part of the lesson features a hands-on activity involving Teachable Machines Image Experiments. Students will witness demonstrations of the "Rock, Paper, Scissors" and "Cats vs Dogs" image experiments, serving as tangible instances of machine learning applications.

Next, the lesson delves into data visualization in Python, emphasizing its importance in today's data-driven world. Students will be shown how to create a bar chart using a list of values, leveraging Python's native capabilities.

The lesson then transitions to reading data from CSV (Comma Separated Values) files, a popular format for data storage and exchange. Students will learn how to read data from a CSV file using Python's built-in `open` function. Furthermore, the lesson introduces the `with open` statement, a best practice for efficient file handling, ensuring that the file is properly closed after its suite finishes execution.

The practical application segment of the lesson focuses on creating a bar chart from CSV data. Students will be tasked with creating a bar chart that depicts the number of medals won by different teams, with the data sourced from a CSV file. They will code along to complete this task, and the resulting output and challenges faced during this process will be discussed, allowing for constructive learning.

Lastly, the lesson concludes with a comprehensive review of the key points covered, along with a Q&A session, ensuring the students have a clear understanding of all the topics taught and their queries are addressed.

Detailed Lesson Notes:

1. Begin the lesson by introducing the concept of machine learning, a type of artificial intelligence that provides computers with the ability to learn without being explicitly programmed. Machine learning focuses on the development of computer programs that can change when exposed to new data.

2. Distinguish between supervised and unsupervised learning. In supervised learning, we teach or train the machine using data which is well-labeled. In unsupervised learning, the machine is provided with a data set and must find patterns and relationships therein.

3. Show students how to use Teachable Machines[1] for image recognition tasks. Discuss how this type of machine learning application can be used in real-world scenarios, such as recognizing gestures in a game of "Rock, Paper, Scissors," or distinguishing between images of cats and dogs.

4. Introduce the concept of data visualization and its importance in interpreting and presenting data. Show students how to create a basic bar chart using Python. The following code creates a bar chart using matplotlib.pyplot. It uses a dictionary to store the data, where the keys are the labels for the bars and the values are the heights of the bars. The ax.bar function is used to create the bars, and plt.show is used to render and display the chart.

PYTHON CODE

```
# Import the matplotlib module for creating visualizations
import matplotlib.pyplot as plt
# Initialize a dictionary with colors as keys and their
corresponding values
```

---

1 https://teachablemachine.withgoogle.com

```python
data = {
    'Blue': 2399,
    'Red': 1413,
    'Green': 1304,
}

# Create a bar chart by calling the bar function on a
subplot object
fig, ax = plt.subplots()
ax.bar(data.keys(), data.values())
# Set the title of the chart
ax.set_title('My Chart')

# Render and display the chart
plt.show()
```

PYTHON OUTPUT

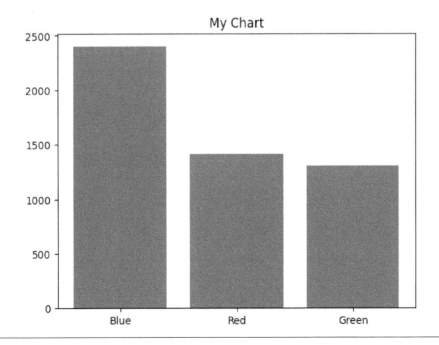

5. Explain the concept of CSV files and how they are used to store data. Show students how to read data from a CSV file using Python's built-in `open` function.

PYTHON CODE

```python
f=open('Medals.csv')
for line in f:

    print(line)
f.close()
```

PYTHON OUTPUT

```
Country,Medals
Afghanistan,15
Algeria,23
Argentina,72
Armenia,17
Australasia,9
Australia,364
Austria,83
Azerbaijan,28
...
```

Alternatively, demonstrate how to use the `with open` statement for more efficient file handling.

PYTHON CODE

```python
with open('Medals.csv') as f:
    for line in f:
    print(line)
```

PYTHON OUTPUT

```
Country,Medals
Afghanistan,15
Algeria,23
Argentina,72
Armenia,17
Australasia,9
Australia,364
Austria,83
Azerbaijan,28
```

6. Finally, guide students through a practical application: creating a bar chart from data sourced from a CSV file. This task will combine students' understanding of data visualization and file handling in Python.

PYTHON CODE

```python
# We start by importing the necessary libraries.
# matplotlib.pyplot is used for making the bar plot.
# csv is used for reading the data from the CSV file.
import matplotlib.pyplot as plt
import csv
```

```python
# We initialize two empty lists where we'll store our team names
# and medal counts.
teams = []
medals = []

# We open the CSV file that contains our data. The 'with' keyword
# ensures the file is properly closed after it is no longer needed.
with open('Medals.csv') as f:
    # We create a CSV reader object which will allow us to
    # iterate over lines in the CSV file.
    csv_reader = csv.reader(f)
    # We skip the header row in the CSV file as we're only
    # interested in the data.
    next(csv_reader)
    # We iterate over each line in the CSV file.
    for line in csv_reader:
        # We store the team name and medal count in their
        # respective lists.
        team = line[0]
        medal = int(line[1])  # We convert the medal count
        # from a string to an integer.
        teams.append(team)
        medals.append(medal)

# We sort the teams and medals lists based on the number of
# medals in ascending order.
# We use the zip() function to pair each team with its
# corresponding medal count, then sort these pairs.
# Finally, we use zip() again to get our sorted teams and
# medals lists.
medals, teams = zip(*sorted(zip(medals, teams)))
```

```python
# We only want the top 10 teams, so we select the last 10 elements
# from our sorted teams and medals lists.
top_teams = teams[-10:]
top_medals = medals[-10:]

# We create a new figure in matplotlib.
plt.figure(figsize=[10,8])

# We create a bar chart with our top 10 teams and their respective
# medal counts.
# We also set the color of the bars and their width.
plt.bar(top_teams, top_medals, color='blue', width=0.6)

# We set the title of our plot and the labels for our
# x and y axes.
plt.title('Top 10 Teams by Medals', fontsize=20)
plt.ylabel('Medal Count', fontsize=14)
plt.xlabel('Team', fontsize=14)

# We set the font size of our x and y ticks and rotate the x ticks
# by 45 degrees for better readability.
plt.xticks(fontsize=12, rotation=45)
plt.yticks(fontsize=12)

# Finally, we use plt.show() to display our plot.
plt.show()
```

PYTHON OUTPUT

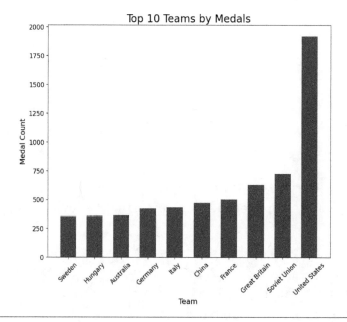

7. Review the key points of the lesson, emphasizing the importance of machine learning and data visualization in Python. Invite questions and feedback from the students to ensure comprehension.

LESSON 10.
INTRODUCTION TO PANDAS –
SERIES AND DATAFRAMES

Lesson Objectives:

The aim of this lesson is to acquaint students with the Pandas library in Python, which offers robust tools for data manipulation and analysis. Throughout the lesson, students will learn about key components of Pandas like Series and DataFrames, comprehend how to import data from CSV files, and delve into data exploration and manipulation methods. The ultimate objective is to enable students to handle, analyze, and transform data efficiently using the Pandas library.

Lesson Plan:

I. Introduction to Pandas

    A. Discussing the importance of data manipulation and analysis in programming

    B. Introducing the Pandas library and its capabilities

    C. Explaining the advantages of using Pandas for data manipulation and analysis tasks

II. Creating Series and DataFrames

    A. Explaining the concept of a Series and its characteristics

    B. Demonstrating the creation of a Series using Pandas' `Series()` function

    C. Introducing the concept of a DataFrame and its advantages over Series

    D. Showing how to create a DataFrame from a dictionary using Pandas' `DataFrame()` function

    E. Discussing the importance of index labels in DataFrames and how to set custom index labels

III. Reading and Analyzing Data

    A. Explaining how to read data from a CSV file using Pandas' `read_csv()` function

B. Demonstrating how to handle common issues with CSV files, such as specifying delimiter and handling missing values

C. Introducing essential DataFrame methods for exploring and analyzing data:
   1. `head()` and `tail()` – displaying the first or last few rows of the DataFrame
   2. `info()` – providing information about the DataFrame's structure, columns, and data types
   3. `shape` – retrieving the dimensions of the DataFrame (rows, columns)
   4. `columns` – accessing the column names of the DataFrame
   5. `isnull()` and `isnull().sum()` – identifying missing values and calculating their count per column

IV. Data Manipulation and Transformation

A. Demonstrating common data manipulation operations using Pandas methods:
   1. `lower()` – converting column names to lowercase for consistency
   2. `filter()` – selecting specific columns based on conditions
   3. `sort_values()` – sorting the DataFrame based on one or more columns

B. Explaining the benefits of chaining methods to perform multiple operations in a concise manner

C. Discussing the concept of method chaining and its syntax using Pandas

V. Review and Q&A

A. Summarizing the key concepts covered in the lesson, including Series, DataFrames, reading CSV files, and data manipulation using Pandas methods

B. Addressing any questions or concerns from the students

C. Encouraging further exploration of Pandas through additional resources and practice exercises

Lesson Description:

The lesson kicks off with an overview of the significance of data manipulation and analysis in programming. The spotlight is then on the Pandas library, a powerhouse in Python for data manipulation and analysis, providing an explanation of its broad capabilities. Here, students will get insights into the advantages of using Pandas, such as efficient data handling, high performance, and varied functionalities.

Following this, we step into the core of the lesson: the creation of Series and DataFrames. A Series, a one-dimensional labeled array, is introduced, outlining its primary characteristics. Creation of a Series using the Pandas' `Series()` function will be demonstrated. The concept of a DataFrame, a versatile, two-dimensional labeled data structure, follows next. Students will learn the benefits of using a DataFrame over a Series, such as its ability to handle heterogeneous data and provide more complex manipulations. The process of creating a DataFrame from a dictionary using the Pandas' `DataFrame()` function will be demonstrated. Here, the significance of index labels in DataFrames and how to set custom index labels will be discussed.

In addition to this, the lesson will delve into the concept of DataFrame indexing. The ability to select and manipulate data is one of the most powerful features of a DataFrame. Indexing in DataFrames can be done in two ways: from 0 (like lists) or from -1 (the end towards the beginning). An integral part of DataFrame manipulation, both these methods of indexing allow the easy selection of data subsets for further analysis and operations.

The journey then leads to the process of reading and analyzing data. Students will be shown how to import data from a CSV file using the Pandas' `read_csv()` function. The session also tackles how to overcome common issues with CSV files, such as delimiter specification and handling missing values. Key DataFrame methods for exploring and analyzing data, including `head()`, `tail()`, `info()`, `shape`, `columns`, `isnull()`, and `isnull().sum()`, will be introduced. These methods facilitate quick data overview, structural insights, dimension retrieval, column name access, and missing value detection.

The next phase of the lesson deals with data manipulation and transformation. Students will experience the transformative abilities of Pandas firsthand, as it shapes raw data into analysis-friendly formats. Methods like `lower()`, `filter()`, and `sort_values()` will be demonstrated, showcasing how to convert column names to lowercase, select columns based on certain conditions, and sort the DataFrame respectively. The advantage of chaining these methods to perform multiple operations succinctly will be emphasized. The concept of method chaining, a technique that enhances both code readability and performance, will be expounded upon using Pandas.

Wrapping up, the lesson concludes with a detailed recap of the concepts covered, including Series, DataFrames, indexing, reading CSV files, and data manipulation using Pandas. A Q&A segment will ensure a clear understanding of the material, resolving any questions or doubts. Encouragement for further exploration of Pandas through additional resources and practice exercises will be extended.

Detailed Lesson Notes:

I. Introduction to Pandas

- Discuss the importance of data manipulation and analysis in programming, emphasizing the need for efficient tools to handle large datasets.
- Introduce the Pandas library and its capabilities:
  - Pandas is an open-source library built on top of NumPy, providing data structures and functions for efficient data manipulation and analysis.
  - Mention its popularity in data science and its extensive use in various domains, such as finance, research, and business analytics.

- Explain that Pandas excels in handling structured, tabular data, similar to spreadsheets or SQL tables.
- Highlight the advantages of Pandas, such as its flexibility, speed, and vast array of functions for data cleaning, transformation, and analysis.

II. Creating Series and DataFrames

- Explain the concept of a Series and its characteristics:
  - A Series is a one-dimensional labeled array that can hold any data type.
  - It consists of data values and associated index labels that uniquely identify each value.
- Demonstrate the creation of a Series using Pandas' `Series()` function:

PYTHON CODE

```python
import pandas as pd
series = pd.Series([10, 20, 30, 40])
```

- Introduce the concept of a DataFrame and its advantages over Series:

- A DataFrame is a two-dimensional labeled data structure, similar to a table in a relational database.
- It allows for storing and manipulating structured data with multiple columns and rows.
- Show how to create a DataFrame from a dictionary using Pandas' `DataFrame()` function:

PYTHON CODE

```python
data = {'apples': [3, 2, 0, 1], 'oranges': [0, 3, 7, 2]}
purchases = pd.DataFrame(data)
```

- Discuss the importance of index labels in DataFrames and how to set custom index labels:

PYTHON CODE

```python
purchases = pd.DataFrame(data, index=['Alex', 'Kirin',
'Lily', 'John'])
```

III. Reading and Analyzing Data

- Explain how to read data from a CSV file using Pandas' `read_csv()` function:

PYTHON CODE

```python
df = pd.read_csv('data.csv')
```

- Demonstrating how to handle common issues with CSV files, such as specifying the delimiter and handling missing values:

PYTHON CODE

```python
df = pd.read_csv('data.csv', delimiter=',', na_values='NaN')
```

- Introduce essential DataFrame methods for exploring and analyzing data:
  - `head()` and `tail()` – display the first or last few rows of the DataFrame:

PYTHON CODE

```python
df.head()
```

PYTHON OUTPUT

	data1	data2	data3	data4
0	11.0	16.0	20.0	22.0
1	24.0	NaN	19.0	14.0
2	8.0	NaN	2.0	12.0
3	3.0	4.0	24.0	20.0
4	19.0	28.0	7.0	3.0

```
df.tail()
```

	data1	data2	data3	data4
25	13.0	29.0	12.0	22.0
26	NaN	28.0	7.0	6.0
27	NaN	12.0	30.0	8.0
28	4.0	12.0	12.0	23.0
29	4.0	1.0	NaN	26.0

- `info()` – provide information about the DataFrame's structure, columns, and data types:

```
df.info()
```

```
<class 'pandas.core.frame.DataFrame'>
RangeIndex: 30 entries, 0 to 29
Data columns (total 4 columns):
 #   Column  Non-Null Count  Dtype
---  ------  --------------  -----
 0   data1   26 non-null     float64
 1   data2   26 non-null     float64
 2   data3   26 non-null     float64
 3   data4   26 non-null     float64
```

```
dtypes: float64(4)
memory usage: 1.1 KB
```

- `shape` – retrieve the dimensions of the DataFrame (rows, columns):

PYTHON CODE

```
df.shape
```

PYTHON OUTPUT

```
(30, 4)
```

- `columns` – access the column names of the DataFrame:

PYTHON CODE

```
df.columns
```

PYTHON OUTPUT

```
Index(['data1', 'data2', 'data3', 'data4'], dtype='object')
```

- `isnull()` and `isnull().sum()` – identify missing values and calculate their count per column:

PYTHON CODE

```
df.isnull()
```

PYTHON OUTPUT

	data1	data2	data3	data4
0	False	False	False	False
1	False	True	False	False
2	False	True	False	False
3	False	False	False	False
4	False	False	False	False
5	False	False	False	False
6	True	True	True	False
7	False	False	True	False
8	False	False	False	False
9	False	False	False	False
10	False	False	False	False
11	False	False	False	True
12	False	False	False	False
13	False	False	False	False
14	False	True	False	True
15	False	False	False	False
16	False	False	False	False
17	False	False	True	False

18	False	False	False	False
19	True	False	False	False
20	False	False	False	True
21	False	False	False	False
22	False	False	False	False
23	False	False	False	True
24	False	False	False	False
25	False	False	False	False
26	True	False	False	False
27	True	False	False	False
28	False	False	False	False
29	False	False	True	False

PYTHON CODE

```
df.isnull().sum()
```

PYTHON OUTPUT

```
data1    4
data2    4
data3    4
data4    4
dtype:   int64
```

IV. Data Manipulation and Transformation

- Demonstrate common data manipulation operations using Pandas methods:
  - `lower()` – convert column names to lowercase for consistency:

PYTHON CODE

```python
df.columns = [col.lower() for col in df.columns]
```

- `filter()` – select specific columns based on conditions:

PYTHON CODE

```python
filtered_df = df.filter(['data1', 'data22'])
filtered_df.head()
```

PYTHON OUTPUT

	data1
0	11.0
1	24.0
2	8.0
3	3.0
4	19.0

- `sort_values()` – sort the DataFrame based on one or more columns:

PYTHON CODE

```python
sorted_df = df.sort_values(by=['data1', 'data2'], ascending=False)
sorted_df.head()
```

PYTHON OUTPUT

	data1	data2	data3	data4
22	30.0	9.0	3.0	22.0
5	28.0	27.0	1.0	6.0
14	26.0	NaN	2.0	NaN
8	25.0	14.0	24.0	22.0
1	24.0	NaN	19.0	14.0

- Explain the benefits of chaining methods to perform multiple operations in a concise manner:

PYTHON CODE

```python
filtered_sorted_df = df.filter(['data1', 'data2']).sort_
values(by='data1', ascending=False)
filtered_sorted_df.head()
```

PYTHON OUTPUT

	data1	data2
22	30.0	9.0
5	28.0	27.0
14	26.0	NaN
8	25.0	14.0
1	24.0	NaN

V. Review and Q&A

- Summarize the key concepts covered in the lesson, including Series, DataFrames, reading CSV files, and data manipulation using Pandas methods.

- Address any questions or concerns from the students regarding the lesson content or Pandas in general.

- Encourage students to explore Pandas further through additional resources, documentation, and practice exercises.

LESSON 11.
MORE PANDAS

Lesson Objectives:

The primary objectives of this lesson are to familiarize students with practical applications of the Python libraries: Pandas, Numpy, Seaborn, Matplotlib.pyplot, BeautifulSoup, and Requests. It will help students comprehend how to merge, explore, analyze, and visualize data using these libraries, working with real-world datasets. Furthermore, the lesson aims to introduce students to web scraping and data extraction from webpages. The overall goal is to empower students with hands-on experience, translating theoretical concepts into concrete, actionable knowledge.

Lesson Plan:

I.   Olympic Medals Analysis using Pandas

    A. Importing the necessary libraries: pandas, numpy, seaborn, matplotlib.pyplot

    B. Reading the medals and population data from CSV files using Pandas' `read_csv()` function

    C. Merging the two dataframes based on the country index using `merge()`

    D. Performing data exploration and analysis:

        1. Using `info()` to get information about the merged dataframe

        2. Creating a new column 'Normalized' to calculate normalized medals per million population

        3. Resetting the index of the dataframe using `reset_index()`

        4. Visualizing the normalized medals using a bar plot with seaborn's `barplot()` function and matplotlib.pyplot's `show()` function

II. Jail Break Analysis

    A. Web scraping using BeautifulSoup to extract data from a Wikipedia page

B. Defining a helper function `data_from_url()` to fetch data from a URL using requests and BeautifulSoup
C. Calling `data_from_url()` to fetch the jail break data from the Wikipedia page
D. Performing data exploration and analysis:
  1. Using `info()` to get information about the extracted data
  2. Converting the 'Date' column to datetime format using `pd.to_datetime()`
  3. Visualizing the number of prison escapes per year using a bar plot with matplotlib.pyplot's `plot()` function
  4. Visualizing the number of prison escapes per country and prison using bar plots with matplotlib.pyplot's `plot()` function

Lesson Description:

Our lesson begins with an engaging data analysis project: 'Olympic Medals Analysis using Pandas.' Students will learn to import the necessary Python libraries, such as Pandas for data handling, Numpy for numerical operations, Seaborn and Matplotlib.pyplot for data visualization. Students will then read two CSV files containing medals and population data using the Pandas `read_csv()` function. Next, they will merge these dataframes using the `merge()` function, indexing by country. A vital feature of Pandas, `merge()`, allows for easy combination of dataframes based on a common key.

Moving on, students will perform data exploration and analysis. They will use the `info()` method to obtain insights about the merged dataframe, such as data types, non-null values, and memory usage. To facilitate the analysis, a new column 'Normalized' will be created, calculating medals per million population, to provide a fair comparison across countries. Students will learn the `reset_index()` method to modify the dataframe's index. Subsequently, they will visualize the normalized medals using Seaborn's `barplot()` function, showcasing the power of data visualization in deriving meaningful insights.

Transitioning to the second part of the lesson, 'Jail Break Analysis,' students will be introduced to the fascinating world of web scraping. We will import BeautifulSoup, a Python library for parsing HTML and XML documents, and Requests, a popular library for sending HTTP requests. A helper function, `data_from_url()`, will be defined to fetch data from a URL using these libraries. Students will apply this function to extract jail break data from a Wikipedia page.

Further data exploration and analysis will ensue. Similar to the previous project, the `info()` function will be employed to understand the extracted data. Then, the 'Date' column will be converted to a datetime format using `pd.to_datetime()`, a crucial technique for handling date-time data. Students will then visualize the number of prison escapes per year using a bar plot, harnessing the `plot()` function from Matplotlib.pyplot.

Lastly, students will create two additional bar plots to visualize the number of prison escapes per country and per prison, further extending their skills in data manipulation and visualization.

Concluding the lesson, we will recap the methodologies and functions learned during the analysis of both datasets. Students will be encouraged to explore further applications of the libraries and methods used, with additional resources and exercises provided for practice. A Q&A session will address any outstanding queries, ensuring a comprehensive understanding of the topics covered.

Detailed Lesson Notes:

I.   Olympic Medals Analysis using Pandas

1. Import the necessary libraries and explain their purposes:

PYTHON CODE

```python
import pandas as pd   # For data manipulation and analysis
import numpy as np   # For numerical operations
import seaborn as sns   # For data visualization
import matplotlib.pyplot as plt   # For creating plots and charts
```

---

2. Read the medals and population data from CSV files using Pandas' `read_csv()` function:

PYTHON CODE

```python
df = pd.read_csv("Medals.csv", index_col='Country')
df1 = pd.read_csv("Population.csv", index_col='Country')
```

---

3. Merge the two dataframes based on the country index using the `merge()` function:

PYTHON CODE

```
df2 = df.merge(df1, left_index=True, right_index=True)
```

4. Perform data exploration and analysis. In the following code:

PYTHON CODE

```
df2.sort_values(by='Medals', ascending=False).reset_
index(drop=True):
```
This line sorts the DataFrame in descending order by the 'Medals' column and resets the index. The drop=True parameter is used to avoid setting the old index as a new column.

```
df_top10 = df2.head(10):
```
This line creates a new DataFrame that only includes the top 10 rows from the sorted DataFrame.

```
sns.barplot(x='Country', y='Normalized', data=df_top10):
```
This line creates a bar plot using the 'df_top10' DataFrame.

```
plt.xticks(rotation=45, ha='right')
```
is used to rotate the x-axis labels by 45 degrees, and the ha='right' parameter is used to align the labels to the right.

```
# Display information about the merged dataframe
df2.info()
```

```
# Calculate normalized medals per million population
df2['Normalized'] = df2['Medals'] / df2['Population']*1000000
```

```python
# Sort the DataFrame by 'Medals' column in descending order and
reset the index
df2 = df2.sort_values(by='Medals', ascending=False).reset_
index(drop=False)

# Create a new DataFrame 'df_top10' that only contains the top
10 countries
df_top10 = df2.head(10)

# Create a bar plot of normalized medals using seaborn
sns.barplot(x='Country', y='Normalized', data=df_top10)

# Rotate x-axis labels for better visibility
plt.xticks(rotation=45, ha='right')

# Display the plot using matplotlib.pyplot
plt.show()
```

PYTHON OUTPUT

```
<class 'pandas.core.frame.DataFrame'>
RangeIndex: 132 entries, 0 to 131
Data columns (total 4 columns):
 #   Column      Non-Null Count  Dtype
---  ------      --------------  -----
 0   Country     132 non-null    object
 1   Medals      132 non-null    int64
 2   Population  132 non-null    int64
 3   Normalized  132 non-null    float64
dtypes: float64(1), int64(2), object(1)
memory usage: 4.2+ KB
```

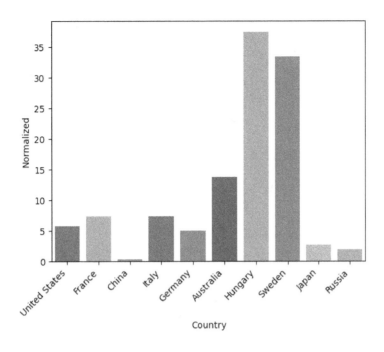

II. Jail Break Analysis

1. Perform web scraping using BeautifulSoup to extract data from a Wikipedia page[1]:

PYTHON CODE

```
import pandas as pd  # For data manipulation and analysis
import requests  # For making HTTP requests
import bs4 import BeautifulSoup  # For web scraping
```

---

1 https://en.wikipedia.org/wiki/List_of_helicopter_prison_escapes

```python
def data_from_url(url, tag_name, class_name):
    response = requests.get(url)
    if response.status_code != 200:
        print('HTTP 404: Page not found')
    else:
        soup = BeautifulSoup(response.text, 'html.parser')
        # Create a BeautifulSoup object
        html_output = soup.find(tag_name, {'class': class_name})
        # Find the specified HTML element using class name
        output = pd.read_html(str(html_output))
        # Extract data tables from HTML
    return output[0]  # Return the first extracted table
as a DataFrame
```

2. Call the `data_from_url()` function to fetch the jail break data from the Wikipedia page:

PYTHON CODE

```python
escape_data = data_from_url("https://en.wikipedia.org/wiki/List_of_helicopter_prison_escapes", "table", "wikitable")
```

3. Perform data exploration and analysis:

PYTHON CODE

```python
escape_data.info()  # Display information about the extracted data
```

```python
escape_data['Date'] = pd.to_datetime(escape_data['Date'])  # Convert
the 'Date' column to datetime format
escape_year_plot = escape_data['Date'].dt.year.value_counts().
plot(kind='bar', xlabel='Year', ylabel='No. of Escapes',
title='Prison Breaks Per Year', figsize=(12, 6))  # Create a bar plot
of prison breaks per year
plt.show()  # Display the plot using matplotlib.pyplot
escape_country_plot = escape_data['Country'].value_counts().
plot(kind='bar', xlabel='Country', ylabel='No. of Escapes',
title='Prison Breaks per Country', figsize=(12, 6))  # Create a bar
plot of prison breaks per country
plt.show()  # Display the plot using matplotlib.pyplot
escape_name_plot = escape_data['Prison name'].value_counts().
plot(kind='bar', xlabel='Prison name', ylabel='No. of Escapes',
title='Prison Breaks per Prison', figsize=(12, 6))  # Create a bar
plot of prison breaks per prison
plt.show()  # Display the plot using matplotlib.pyplot
```

PYTHON OUTPUT

```
<class 'pandas.core.frame.DataFrame'>
RangeIndex: 48 entries, 0 to 47
Data columns (total 6 columns):
 #   Column        Non-Null Count  Dtype
---  ------        --------------  -----
 0   Date          48 non-null     object
 1   Prison name   48 non-null     object
 2   Country       48 non-null     object
 3   Succeeded     48 non-null     object
 4   Escapee(s)    48 non-null     object
 5   Details       48 non-null     object
dtypes: object(6)
memory usage: 2.4+ KB
```

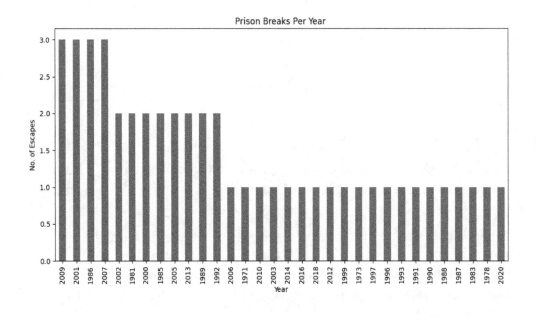

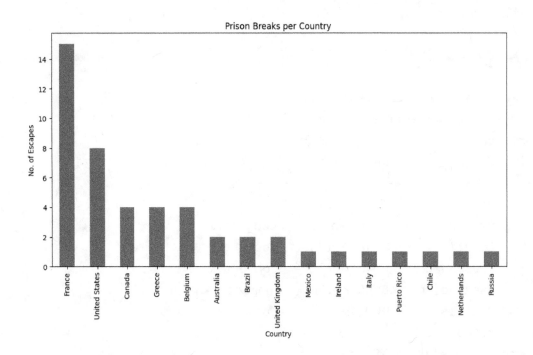

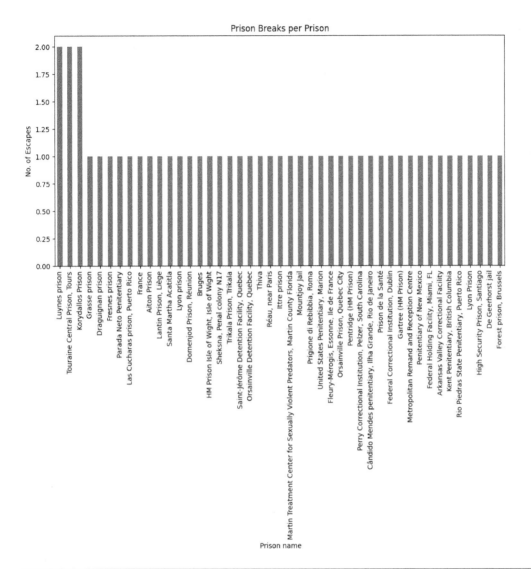

Prison Breaks per Prison

LESSON 12. PRACTICE TEST – MANIPULATING DATAFRAMES

Lesson Objectives:

This practice test aims to provide students with hands-on practice with key Python libraries and data structures, specifically focusing on operations with Pandas' DataFrames. The test will cover DataFrame creation, renaming and dropping columns, selecting specific rows and columns, data type conversions, correlation calculations, and missing values detection. It also includes a bonus task to enhance string manipulation skills. The overall objective is to reinforce students' understanding of Python's data handling capabilities, preparing them for more complex data analysis tasks.

Lesson Plan:

I. Task 1: Creating and Printing a DataFrame

A. Creating a DataFrame with specific column names and values

B. Printing the first few rows of the DataFrame

II. Task 2: Printing Info about DataFrame

A. Using the `info()` method to obtain information about the DataFrame

III. Task 3: Renaming a Column

A. Renaming a column in the DataFrame using the `rename()` method

B. Printing the updated list of columns

IV. Task 4: Creating a DataFrame without a Column

A. Creating a new DataFrame without a specific column using the `drop()` method

B. Printing the first few rows of the new DataFrame

V. Task 5: Creating a DataFrame with Specific Columns

A. Creating a new DataFrame with only specific columns using the `iloc` indexer

B. Printing the first few rows of the new DataFrame

VI. Task 6: Creating a DataFrame with Specific Rows

A. Creating a new DataFrame with only specific rows using the `iloc` indexer

B. Printing the first few rows of the new DataFrame

VII. Task 7: Converting DataFrame Data Types

A. Converting the data types of the DataFrame using the `astype()` method

B. Printing the updated information about the DataFrame

VIII. Task 8: Computing Correlations in DataFrame

A. Calculating correlations between columns in the DataFrame using the `corr()` method

B. Printing the correlation matrix

IX. Task 9: Checking DataFrame for Missing Values

A. Checking the DataFrame for missing values using the `isna()` method

B. Summing the missing values for each column

X. Bonus Task: Removing Duplicates from a String

    A. Implementing a function to remove duplicates from a given string

    B. Applying the function to a specific string and printing the result

XI. Review and Q&A

    A. Reviewing the key concepts covered in the practice test

    B. Addressing any questions or doubts from students

Lesson Description:

The practice test begins with the task of creating a DataFrame with specified column names and values. Students will use the `DataFrame()` method from Pandas, an invaluable Python library known for its strong data manipulation abilities. They will understand how to construct a DataFrame from a dictionary, with keys and values serving as column names and data, respectively.

In Task 2, students will employ the `info()` method on the DataFrame. This method presents a concise summary of the

DataFrame, including information about the index dtype and column dtypes, non-null values, and memory usage.

Next, Task 3 covers column renaming in a DataFrame using the `rename()` method. This method is crucial in DataFrame manipulation as it allows for easier readability and understanding of the data. Students will learn to print the updated list of columns to verify the changes.

In Task 4, students will explore the `drop()` method to create a new DataFrame without a specific column. This method demonstrates the ease of removing unwanted data from a DataFrame. They will learn to print the first few rows of the new DataFrame for validation.

Task 5 & 6 introduce the `iloc` indexer to create new DataFrames with only specific columns and rows, respectively. The `iloc` indexer offers simple and efficient data selection based on integer-location.

In Task 7, students will learn the importance of handling data types in Python using the `astype()` method. By converting the data types of DataFrame columns, students can perform appropriate computations on the data.

Task 8 involves computing correlations between DataFrame columns using the `corr()` method. This provides insightful information about the relationships between different data elements.

In Task 9, students will check the DataFrame for missing values using the `isna()` method. This method identifies any gaps in the data that could affect further analysis. The practice test also reinforces the concept of chaining methods in Python, as students will sum the missing values for each column.

The practice test concludes with a Bonus Task involving string manipulation. Students will implement a function to remove duplicates from a given string, practicing string handling skills in Python.

The practice test wraps up with a comprehensive review of the key concepts covered, followed by a Q&A session to address students' queries and doubts. Through this practice test, students will gain practical experience in DataFrame manipulation, string handling, and error detection, enhancing their Python proficiency.

Detailed Lesson Notes:

I. Task 1: Creating and Printing a DataFrame

- Explain the task: Create a DataFrame with 4 rows and 5 columns, where the column names are 'col1', 'col2', 'col3', 'col4', 'col5', and the values are strings containing numbers from 1 to 20.
- Solution code to create the DataFrame:

PYTHON CODE

```python
df = pd.DataFrame([['1', '2', '3', '4', '5'],
                   ['6', '7', '8', '9', '10'],
                   ['11', '12', '13', '14', '15'],
                   ['16', '17', '18', '19', '20']],
                  columns=['cl1', 'col2', 'col3', 'col4', 'col5'])
```

- Print the first five rows of the DataFrame using the `head()` method:

PYTHON CODE

```python
df.head()
```

---

	cl1	col2	col3	col4	col5
0	1	2	3	4	5
1	6	7	8	9	10
2	11	12	13	14	15
3	16	17	18	19	20

II. Task 2: Printing Info about DataFrame

- Explain the task: Print information about the DataFrame, including the types of entries and the number of entries.
- Solution code to print the information:

PYTHON CODE

```
df.info()
```

PYTHON OUTPUT

```
<class 'pandas.core.frame.DataFrame'>
RangeIndex: 4 entries, 0 to 3
Data columns (total 5 columns):
 #   Column  Non-Null Count  Dtype
---  ------  --------------  -----
 0   cl1     4 non-null      object
 1   col2    4 non-null      object
 2   col3    4 non-null      object
```

```
3    col4    4 non-null        object
4    col5    4 non-null        object
dtypes: object(5)
memory usage: 288.0+ bytes
```

III. Task 3: Renaming a Column

- Explain the task: Rename the column 'cl1' to 'col1' in the DataFrame.
- Solution code to rename the column using the `rename()` method:

PYTHON CODE

```
df.rename(columns={'cl1': 'col1'}, inplace=True)
```

- Print the updated list of columns:

PYTHON CODE

```
df.columns
```

PYTHON OUTPUT

```
Index(['col1', 'col2', 'col3', 'col4', 'col5'], dtype='object')
```

IV. Task 4: Creating a DataFrame without a Column

- Explain the task: Create a new DataFrame `X` that contains all the data from the original DataFrame `df`, except for the column 'col1'.
- Solution code to create the new DataFrame using the `drop()` method:

PYTHON CODE

```python
X = df.drop(['col1'], axis=1)
```

- Print the first few rows of the new DataFrame `X`:

PYTHON CODE

```python
X.head()
```

PYTHON OUTPUT

	col2	col3	col4	col5
0	2	3	4	5
1	7	8	9	10
2	12	13	14	15
3	17	18	19	20

V. Task 5: Creating a DataFrame with Specific Columns

- Explain the task: Create a new DataFrame `Y` that contains only the data from columns 'col3' and 'col4' from the original DataFrame `df`.
- Solution code to create the new DataFrame using the `iloc` indexer:

PYTHON CODE

```python
Y = df.iloc[:, 2:4]
```

- Print the first few rows of the new DataFrame `Y`:

PYTHON CODE

```python
Y.head()
```

PYTHON OUTPUT

	col3	col4
0	3	4
1	8	9
2	13	14
3	18	19

VI. Task 6: Creating a DataFrame with Specific Rows

- Explain the task: Create a new DataFrame `Z` that contains only the data from rows 2 and 3 from the original DataFrame `df`.
- Solution code to create the new DataFrame using the `iloc` indexer:

PYTHON CODE

```python
Z = df.iloc[1:3, :]
```

- Print the first few rows of the new DataFrame `Z`:

PYTHON CODE

```python
Z.head()
```

PYTHON OUTPUT

	col1	col2	col3	col4	col5
1	6	7	8	9	10
2	11	12	13	14	15

VII. Task 7: Converting DataFrame Data Types

- Explain the task: Create a new DataFrame `I` that contains the data from the original DataFrame `df`, but with all the values converted to integers.
- Solution code to convert the data types using the `astype()` method:

PYTHON CODE

```python
I = df.astype('int')
```

,- Print the updated information about the DataFrame `I`:

PYTHON CODE

```python
I.info()
```

PYTHON OUTPUT

```
<class 'pandas.core.frame.DataFrame'>
RangeIndex: 4 entries, 0 to 3
Data columns (total 5 columns):
 #   Column  Non-Null Count  Dtype
---  ------  --------------  -----
 0   col1    4 non-null      int64
 1   col2    4 non-null      int64
 2   col3    4 non-null      int64
```

```
3    col4    4 non-null        int64
4    col5    4 non-null        int64
dtypes: int64(5)
memory usage: 288.0 bytes
```

VIII.   Task 8: Computing Correlations in DataFrame

- Explain the task: Calculate the correlations between columns in the DataFrame `I`.
- Solution code to compute correlations using the `corr()` method:

PYTHON CODE

```
I.corr(method='pearson')
```

PYTHON OUTPUT

	col1	col2	col3	col4	col5
col1	1.0	1.0	1.0	1.0	1.0
col2	1.0	1.0	1.0	1.0	1.0
col3	1.0	1.0	1.0	1.0	1.0
col4	1.0	1.0	1.0	1.0	1.0
col5	1.0	1.0	1.0	1.0	1.0

IX. Task 9: Checking DataFrame for Missing Values

- Explain the task: Check the DataFrame `df` for missing values and print the sum of missing values for each column.
- Solution code to check for missing values using the `isna()` method and sum the missing values:

PYTHON CODE

```python
df.isna().sum()
```

PYTHON OUTPUT

```
col1    0
col2    0
col3    0
col4    0
col5    0
dtype: int64
```

X. Bonus Task: Removing Duplicates from a String

- Explain the bonus task: Implement a function to remove duplicates from a given string. Apply

the function to the string 'AAABBCDDD' and print the result.
- Solution code to remove duplicates from a string using a function:

PYTHON CODE

```python
def removeDuplicates(s):
    chars = []
    prev = None
    for c in s:
        if prev != c:
            chars.append(c)
            prev = c
    return ''.join(chars)
s = 'AAABBCDDD'
print('String without duplicates:')
print(removeDuplicates(s))
```

PYTHON OUTPUT

```
String without duplicates:
ABCD
```

XI. Review and Q&A

- Summarize the key concepts covered in the practice test and provide an opportunity for students to ask questions and clarify any doubts they may have.

LESSON 13.
MORE ON DATA FRAMES

Lesson Objectives:

The objective of this follow-up lesson is to deepen students' understanding of the Pandas library, focusing specifically on DataFrame creation and manipulation techniques. Students will learn different ways of creating DataFrames, renaming columns and rows, and dropping columns. Additionally, they will be exposed to a range of DataFrame indexing techniques, including selecting specific columns and slicing rows and columns. The ultimate goal is to solidify students' abilities to work efficiently with DataFrames, a foundational skill in data manipulation and analysis.

Lesson Plan:

I. Creating Data Frames

 A. Creating a data frame using a list of lists
 B. Creating a data frame using a dictionary
 C. Creating a data frame with custom index

II. Renaming Columns and Rows

 A. Renaming columns using the `rename()` method
 B. Renaming rows (index) using the `rename()` method
 C. Modifying the index using the `reindex()` method

III. Dropping Columns

 A. Dropping columns using the `drop()` method
 B. Selecting specific columns using indexing
 C. Selecting rows and columns using slicing

Lesson Description:

The lesson begins by exploring various ways to create DataFrames using the Pandas library. First, students will learn to create a DataFrame using a list of lists, where each list represents a row in the DataFrame. Following this, students will be shown how to create a DataFrame from a dictionary, where the dictionary keys and values correspond to column names and their values, respectively. Lastly, the lesson will delve into creating a DataFrame with a custom index, providing students with the ability to label rows in a more meaningful manner.

The next part of the lesson targets renaming columns and rows in a DataFrame. Students will utilize the `rename()` method to change the names of specific columns and rows (indexes). The `rename()` method is instrumental in improving data readability and semantics in a DataFrame. Furthermore, they will learn how to modify the index using the `reindex()` method. The `reindex()` method allows for altering the DataFrame to conform to a new index, demonstrating the flexibility of DataFrames.

The third section of the lesson addresses dropping columns from a DataFrame. Students will employ the `drop()` method to remove specific columns, a necessary technique when dealing with extraneous or irrelevant data. The lesson will also introduce different indexing techniques to select specific columns in a DataFrame. This is a critical skill, as it allows for the extraction of desired data for further analysis.

Expanding on indexing techniques, the lesson will instruct students on selecting rows and columns using slicing. Slicing is a powerful feature in Python that provides a way to retrieve subsets of data. Students will learn how to use slicing on DataFrames, which allows for versatile and efficient data selection.

In conclusion, this lesson strives to build upon students' initial exposure to DataFrame manipulation in the practice test, moving into more intricate aspects of DataFrame operations. A comprehensive understanding of these techniques can greatly enhance data manipulation efficiency, forming a robust foundation for further learning in data analysis.

Detailed Lesson Notes:

1. Creating Data Frames:
   a) Create a data frame using a list of lists:

PYTHON CODE

```
df = pd.DataFrame([['1', '2', '3', '4', '5'],
                   ['6', '7', '8', '9', '10'],
                   ['11', '12', '13', '14', '15'],
                   ['16', '17', '18', '19', '20']],
```

```
                 columns=['col1', 'col2', 'col3', 'col4', 'col5'])

df.head()
```

PYTHON OUTPUT

	col1	col2	col3	col4	col5
0	1	2	3	4	5
1	6	7	8	9	10
2	11	12	13	14	15
3	16	17	18	19	20

---

b) Create a data frame using a dictionary:

PYTHON CODE

```
df1 = pd.DataFrame({'Col1': ['1', '6', '11', '16'],
                    'Col2': ['2', '7', '12', '17'],
                    'Col3': ['3', '8', '13', '18'],
                    'Col4': ['4', '9', '14', '19'],
                    'Col5': ['5', '10', '15', '20']})
df1.head()
```

PYTHON OUTPUT

	Col1	Col2	Col3	Col4	Col5
0	1	2	3	4	5
1	6	7	8	9	10
2	11	12	13	14	15
3	16	17	18	19	20

2. Renaming Columns:

   Renaming columns using the `rename()` method:

PYTHON CODE

```
df.info()
df.rename(columns={'col1': 'Col1'}, inplace=True)
df.columns
```

PYTHON OUTPUT

```
<class 'pandas.core.frame.DataFrame'>
RangeIndex: 4 entries, 0 to 3
Data columns (total 5 columns):
 #   Column  Non-Null Count  Dtype
---  ------  --------------  -----
 0   col1    4 non-null      object
 1   col2    4 non-null      object
 2   col3    4 non-null      object
 3   col4    4 non-null      object
 4   col5    4 non-null      object
dtypes: object(5)
memory usage: 288.0+ bytes
Index(['Col1', 'col2', 'col3', 'col4', 'col5'], dtype='object')
```

---

3. Renaming Rows (Index):

   Renaming rows (index) using the `rename()` method:

PYTHON CODE

```
df.info()
df.rename(index={0: 'Row1'}, inplace=True)
df.index
```

PYTHON OUTPUT

```
Index(['Row1', 1, 2, 3], dtype='object')
```

4. Dropping Columns:
   a) Dropping columns using the `drop()` method:

PYTHON CODE

```
X = df.drop(['Col1'], axis=1)
X.head()
```

PYTHON OUTPUT

	col2	col3	col4	col5
Row1	2	3	4	5
1	7	8	9	10
2	12	13	14	15
3	17	18	19	20

b) Selecting specific columns using slicing and
negative indexing:

PYTHON CODE

```python
Y = df.iloc[:, -3:-1]
Y.head()
```

PYTHON OUTPUT

	col3	col4
Row1	3	4
1	8	9
2	13	14
3	18	19

---

c) Selecting rows and columns using slicing:

PYTHON CODE

```python
Z = df.iloc[2:, :]
Z.head()
```

PYTHON OUTPUT

	Col1	col2	col3	col4	col5
2	11	12	13	14	15
3	16	17	18	19	20

LESSON 14.
MORE ON FOR LOOPS

Lesson Objectives:

The aim of this lesson is to revisit Python's `for` loops, emphasizing the application of iteration techniques in different contexts. Initially, students will recap the basics of `for` loops, including iteration over a string, use of conditional statements, and implementation of `break` and `continue` statements. The lesson will further delve into nested `for` loops and the `zip` function. The next segment will apply these concepts to the Pandas library, demonstrating how to iterate over rows in a DataFrame. Finally, the lesson will introduce the fun and interactive ColabTurtle library, where students will practice their understanding of loops while creating graphical patterns. The objective is to solidify students' comprehension of iteration in Python, thereby enhancing their problem-solving skills.

Lesson Plan:

I.   Refreshing Our Memories

A. Reviewing the basics of for loops

B. Iterating over a string

C. Using conditional statements within for loops

D. Using break and continue statements

E. Nested for loops and the zip function

II.   FOR Loops and Pandas

A. Introduction to pandas library

B. Iterating over rows in a DataFrame using `iterrows()`

C. Accessing values within rows

D. Alternative methods for iterating over rows

III. Let's Have Some Fun with Turtle

A. Installing the ColabTurtle library

B. Basic Turtle movements: drawing squares

C. Creating a spiral pattern

D. Defining a polygon function and using it with Turtle

Lesson Description:

We kick off the lesson with a recap of `for` loop basics, where students will iterate over a string to access individual characters. This revisits the fundamental concept of iteration in Python. They will also learn to incorporate conditional statements within `for` loops, controlling the flow of the loop based on specific conditions.

Continuing with the control statements, students will practice the `break` and `continue` statements. The `break` statement allows for the immediate termination of the loop, while the `continue` statement skips the remainder of the current iteration and moves on to the next. These techniques are essential for controlling the loop's execution based on certain criteria.

The lesson then introduces the concept of nested `for` loops, where one `for` loop is placed inside another. This is particularly useful when dealing with multi-dimensional data structures. Alongside this, students will explore the `zip` function, which allows for simultaneous iteration over multiple sequences.

The second part of the lesson applies these iteration concepts to the Pandas library. Students will learn how to iterate over rows in a DataFrame using the `iterrows()` function, a vital skill in data analysis where often operations must be performed row by row. This section will also cover accessing values within rows and discuss alternative methods for iterating over rows.

The lesson concludes with an engaging exploration of the ColabTurtle library. After installing the library, students will use `for` loops to instruct a turtle to move and create graphical patterns. Initially, they will create a simple square. Then, by extending this concept, they will create a fascinating spiral pattern. Finally, students will define a function to draw a polygon and use it in conjunction with the turtle, reinforcing their understanding of both `for` loops and functions.

This lesson is designed to provide students with a comprehensive understanding of `for` loops and their practical applications, from data manipulation in Pandas to creating graphical designs in ColabTurtle. By intertwining fundamental concepts with engaging activities, students can solidify their knowledge and foster their interest in Python programming.

Detailed Lesson Notes:

1. Refreshing Our Memories:

   a) Reviewing the basics of for loops:

PYTHON CODE

```python
names = ['Dan', 'John', 'Allison', 'Lee', 'Samantha']
print(names)
for name in names:
    print(name)
```

PYTHON OUTPUT

```
['Dan', 'John', 'Allison', 'Lee', 'Samantha']
Dan
John
Allison
Lee
Samantha
```

- The for loop iterates over a list of names and prints each name.

   b) Iterating over a string:

PYTHON CODE

```python
for letter in "This is my string":
    print(letter)
```

PYTHON OUTPUT

```
T
h
i
s

i
s

m
y

s
t
r
i
n
g
```

- The for loop iterates over each character in the
  string and prints it.
  c) Using conditional statements within for loops:

PYTHON CODE

```python
for name in names:
    if name == 'Lee':
        print(name)
```

PYTHON OUTPUT

```
Lee
```

- The for loop iterates over names and prints the name 'Lee' if it is found.
    d) Using break and continue statements:

PYTHON CODE

```python
for name in names:
    print(name)
    if name == 'Allison':
        break
```

PYTHON OUTPUT

```
Dan
John
Allison
```

- The for loop iterates over names, prints each name, and stops when it encounters the name 'Allison'.

PYTHON CODE

```python
for name in names:
    if name == 'Allison':
```

```
        continue
    print(name)
```

PYTHON OUTPUT

```
Dan
John
Lee
Samantha
```

- The for loop iterates over names and skips printing the name 'Allison', but continues with the remaining names.

  e) Nested for loops and the zip function:

PYTHON CODE

```
x = [1, 2, 3]
y = [4, 5, 6]

for i in x:
    for j in y:
        print(str(i) + " " + str(j))
```

PYTHON OUTPUT

```
1 4
1 5
1 6
2 4
```

```
2 5
2 6
3 4
3 5
3 6
```

- The nested for loops iterate over each element in x and y, printing the combination of each pair.

PYTHON CODE

```python
for i, j in zip(x, y):
    print(str(i) + " " + str(j))
```

PYTHON OUTPUT

```
1 4
2 5
3 6
```

- The zip function combines the elements of x and y into pairs, and the for loop iterates over each pair, printing them.

2. FOR Loops and Pandas:

PYTHON CODE

```python
import pandas as pd

df = pd.DataFrame({'c1': [10, 11, 12], 'c2': [100, 110, 120]})
df.reset_index()

for r in df.iterrows():
    print(r)
```

PYTHON OUTPUT

```
(0, c1      10
c2     100
Name: 0, dtype: int64)
(1, c1      11
c2     110
Name: 1, dtype: int64)
(2, c1      12
c2     120
Name: 2, dtype: int64)
```

- The `iterrows()` function iterates over the rows of the DataFrame, returning the index and row as a tuple.

PYTHON CODE

```python
for index, r in df.iterrows():
    print(r[0], r[1])
```

PYTHON OUTPUT

```
10 100
11 110
12 120
```

- The for loop iterates over the rows of the DataFrame, and `r[0]` and `r[1]` access the values in each row.

PYTHON CODE

```python
for index, r in df.iterrows():
    print(r['c1'], r['c2'])
```

PYTHON OUTPUT

```
10 100
11 110
12 120
```

- The for loop iterates over the rows of the DataFrame, and `r['c1']` and `r['c2']` access the values in the specified columns of each row.

PYTHON CODE

```python
for ind in df.index:
    print(df['c1'][ind], df['c2'][ind])
```

PYTHON OUTPUT

```
10 100
11 110
12 120
```

- The for loop iterates over the index of the DataFrame, and `df['c1'][ind]` and `df['c2'][ind]` access the values in the specified columns at each index.

PYTHON CODE

```python
for i in range(len(df)):
    print(df.iloc[i, 0], df.iloc[i, 1])
```

PYTHON OUTPUT

```
10 100
11 110
12 120
```

- The for loop iterates over the range of indices, and `df.iloc[i, 0]` and `df.iloc[i, 1]` access the values in the specified positions of each row using integer indexing.

PYTHON CODE

```
for i in range(len(df)):
    print(df.loc[i, "c1"], df.loc[i, "c2"])
```

PYTHON OUTPUT

```
10 100
11 110
12 120
```

- The for loop iterates over the range of indices, and `df.loc[i, "c1"]` and `df.loc[i, "c2"]` access the values in the specified columns of each row using label indexing.
3. Let's Have Some Fun with Turtle:

PYTHON CODE

```
!pip install colabturtle
# Import the ColabTurtle module. This module allows us to
create a "Lisa" that we can move around the screen to draw
shapes and lines.
import ColabTurtle.Turtle as Lisa
```

```
# Initialize turtle module
Lisa.initializeTurtle()
Lisa.shape("turtle")
# Drawing squares
for x in range(4):
    Lisa.forward(50)
    Lisa.right(90)
```

PYTHON OUTPUT

Looking in indexes: https://pypi.org/simple, https://us-python.pkg.
dev/colab-wheels/public/simple/
Collecting colabturtle
  Downloading ColabTurtle-2.1.0.tar.gz (6.8 kB)
  Preparing metadata (setup.py) ... done
Building wheels for collected packages: colabturtle
  Building wheel for colabturtle (setup.py) ... done
  Created wheel for colabturtle:
filename=ColabTurtle-2.1.0-py3-none-any.whl
size=7642
sha256=
8c49783ca1afc03ce6a798ee48a5566e02b893e8857d708bfc11dddcd8eea6fb
  Stored in directory: /root/.cache/pip/wheels/5b/86/
e8/54f5c8c853606e3a3060bb2e60363cbed632374a12e0f33ffc
Successfully built colabturtle
Installing collected packages: colabturtle
Successfully installed colabturtle-2.1.0
sha256=
8c49783ca1afc03ce6a798ee48a5566e02b893e8857d708bfc11dddcd8eea6fb
  Stored in directory: /root/.cache/pip/wheels/5b/86/
e8/54f5c8c853606e3a3060bb2e60363cbed632374a12e0f33ffc
Successfully built colabturtle
Installing collected packages: colabturtle

Successfully installed colabturtle-2.1.0

- The for loop iterates four times to draw a square using the ColabTurtle graphics library.

PYTHON CODE

```
Lisa.initializeTurtle()
length = 10
angle = 90
for x in range(10):
    Lisa.forward(length + length)
    Lisa.right(angle)
    length = length + 10
```

PYTHON OUTPUT

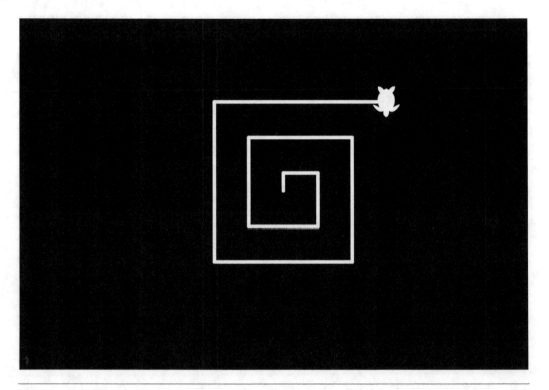

- The for loop iterates ten times to create a spiral pattern using increasing lengths and angles with Turtle.

PYTHON CODE

```python
Lisa.initializeTurtle()
angle = 91
for x in range(100):
    Lisa.forward(x)
    Lisa.left(angle)
```

PYTHON OUTPUT

- The for loop iterates one hundred times to draw a spiral using Turtle, with the length increasing in each iteration.

PYTHON CODE

```
Lisa.initializeTurtle()
def polygon(length, n):
    for _ in range(n):
        Lisa.forward(length)
        Lisa.left(360 / n)
polygon(100, 6)
```

PYTHON OUTPUT

- The `polygon` function defines a regular polygon
  with the given length and number of sides, and the
  for loop uses it to draw a hexagon with Turtle.

LESSON 15.
CLUSTERING WITH K-MEANS

Lesson Objectives:

The primary objective of this lesson is to familiarize students with customer segmentation and clustering techniques, specifically the K-means clustering algorithm. Students will understand the importance of customer segmentation and how clustering can be an effective approach for segmentation. They will get hands-on experience with the K-means clustering algorithm by applying it to a real-world dataset and interpreting the results. Ultimately, the goal is for students to gain practical skills in customer segmentation and data analysis using clustering algorithms.

Lesson Plan:

I. Introduction to Customer Segmentation and Clustering

A. Definition and importance of customer segmentation

B. Overview of clustering as a technique for customer segmentation

C. Introduction to K-means clustering algorithm

II. Loading and Exploring the Dataset

A. Loading the dataset and examining its structure

B. Checking for missing values

C. Visualizing the pairwise relationships and correlations between variables

III. Performing K-means Clustering

A. Preparing the data for clustering

B. Applying K-means clustering algorithm using scikit-learn

C. Assigning cluster labels to the data points

IV. Visualizing the Clusters

A. Using scatter plots and 3D visualization to visualize the clusters

B. Interpretation of the clustering results and analysis of customer behaviors

V.   Review and Q&A

A. Reviewing the key concepts covered in the lesson
B. Addressing any questions or doubts from students

Lesson Description:

The lesson begins by introducing customer segmentation, emphasizing its critical role in enabling businesses to devise tailored strategies to meet specific customer needs. This introduction paves the way for discussing clustering, a type of unsupervised machine learning, which is a popular technique for customer segmentation.

Our focus then shifts to the K-means clustering algorithm. K-means is a centroid-based clustering algorithm where the aim is to minimize the distance between data points and the centroid of the cluster they belong to. Students will be introduced to the iterative process that K-means follows. This process includes:

1. Randomly initializing K centroids.

2. Assigning each data point to the nearest centroid, which forms K clusters.
3. Updating the position of the K centroids to be the mean (average) of all the data points assigned to the respective cluster.
4. Repeating steps 2 and 3 until the centroid positions do not change significantly or a certain number of iterations have been performed.

The trade-offs of using K-means, such as the need to specify the number of clusters beforehand and its sensitivity to the initial centroid positioning, will also be discussed.

Following the theoretical understanding, students will be engaged in a hands-on session where they load a real-world customer dataset using pandas' `read_csv()` function. They will check its structure using methods like `info()` and `describe()` and perform a preliminary visual inspection using seaborn's `pairplot()` and `heatmap()` functions to understand relationships and correlations within the data.

The subsequent segment is dedicated to applying the K-means clustering algorithm on the dataset. The data will first be prepared by normalizing the features using scikit-learn's `StandardScaler()`. This normalization is necessary because K-means is a distance-based algorithm and features on larger scales can unduly influence the result. Next, the K-means clustering algorithm will be applied using scikit-learn's `KMeans()`, and cluster labels will be assigned to the data points.

In the penultimate segment, the students will visualize the clusters formed using matplotlib's `scatter()` function for 2D plots and `Axes3D` for 3D plots. The students will be guided to interpret the clustering results, to identify the distinct customer behaviors represented by each cluster.

The lesson concludes with a review of key concepts ranging from customer segmentation, K-means clustering, to data exploration and visualization. A Q&A session will address any lingering questions or doubts, ensuring the students have a thorough understanding of the practical applications of the K-means algorithm in customer segmentation.

Detailed Lesson Notes:

1. Begin by introducing the concept of customer segmentation and its importance in marketing analytics. Explain that customer segmentation helps identify and

understand different types of customers in order to tailor products or services to their specific needs.

2. Provide an overview of clustering as a technique for customer segmentation. Explain that clustering groups customers based on similarities in their behavior or characteristics.

3. Introduce the K-means clustering algorithm as a popular method for clustering. Explain that K-means aims to partition data points into K clusters by minimizing the sum of squared distances between data points and their cluster centroids.

4. Download the dataset of mall customers[1], import it into dataframe and display the first few rows using the following code:

PYTHON CODE

```
df = pd.read_csv("Mall_Customers.csv")
df.head()
```

---

1 https://www.kaggle.com/datasets/vjchoudhary7/customer-segmentation-tuto-rial-in-python

	CustomerID	Gender	Age	Annual Income (k$)	Spending Score (1-100)
0	1	Male	19	15	39
1	2	Male	21	15	81
2	3	Female	20	16	6
3	4	Female	23	16	77
4	5	Female	31	17	40

5. Explore the dataset by checking its shape, information, and presence of missing values:

PYTHON CODE

```
df.shape
df.info()
df.isna().sum()
```

PYTHON OUTPUT

```
<class 'pandas.core.frame.DataFrame'>
RangeIndex: 200 entries, 0 to 199
Data columns (total 5 columns):
```

#	Column	Non-Null Count	Dtype
0	CustomerID	200 non-null	int64
1	Gender	200 non-null	object
2	Age	200 non-null	int64
3	Annual Income (k$)	200 non-null	int64
4	Spending Score (1-100)	200 non-null	int64

```
dtypes: int64(4), object(1)
memory usage: 7.9+ KB
CustomerID                  0
Gender                      0
Age                         0
Annual Income (k$)          0
Spending Score (1-100)      0
dtype: int64
```

6. Visualize the pairwise relationships and correlations between variables using scatter plots and a heatmap:

PYTHON CODE

```python
# Import the seaborn and matplotlib libraries. Seaborn is a
statistical data visualization library built on top
# of matplotlib. It provides a high-level interface for creating
informative and attractive statistical graphics.
import seaborn as sns
import matplotlib.pyplot as plt


# The pairplot function in seaborn is a convenient tool to
visualize the pairwise relationships and
# distributions of several variables. It creates a grid of Axes
such that each numeric variable in data
# will by shared across the y-axes across a single row and the
x-axes across a single column.
sns.pairplot(df)
```

```python
# The show function in matplotlib is used to display all figures.
It basically opens a window that displays
# the figure and blocks the execution until the window is closed.
plt.show()

# Compute pairwise correlation of columns, excluding NA/null
values using pandas DataFrame corr method.
correlation = df.corr()

# Create a new figure in matplotlib with a defined figsize (10, 8).
plt.figure(figsize=(10, 8))

# The heatmap function in seaborn provides a way to visualize data
in a 2D grid using colors.
# The variable 'correlation' is a matrix in which the (i, j)
element is the correlation between the i-th and j-th variable.
# The parameter 'annot=True' ensures that the values of each cell
appear on the chart.
sns.heatmap(correlation, annot=True)

# Set the title of the current axes in matplotlib.
plt.title("Correlation Heatmap", fontsize=22)

# Again, use the show function in matplotlib to display
all figures.
plt.show()
```

PYTHON OUTPUT

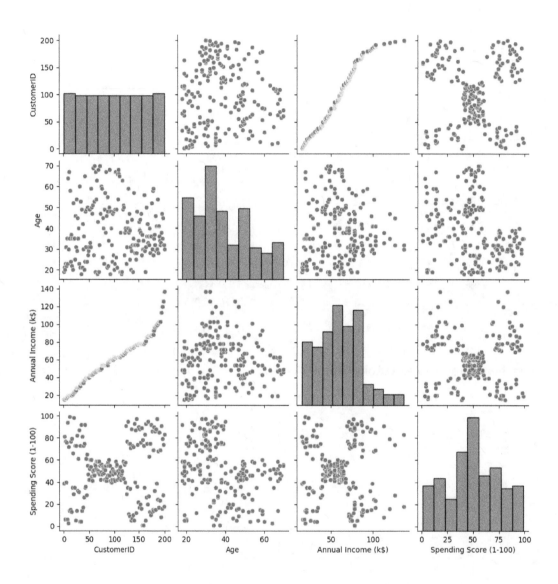

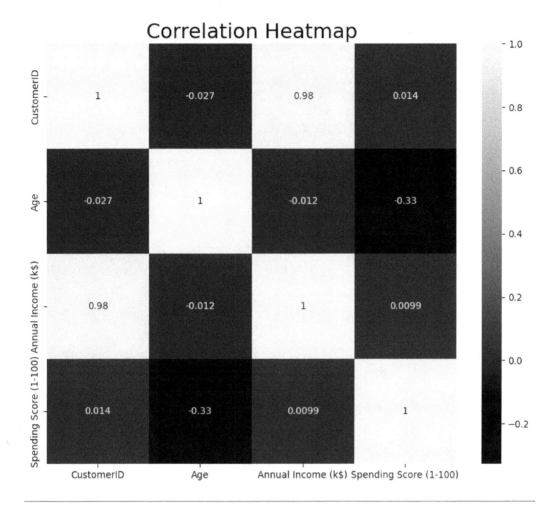

Correlation Heatmap

7. Perform K-means clustering on the dataset using the scikit-learn library:

PYTHON CODE

```
# Import the KMeans class from the sklearn.cluster module. KMeans
is a widely-used clustering algorithm
# that seeks to partition data into k clusters, each represented
by the mean of the data points in the cluster.
```

```python
from sklearn.cluster import KMeans
# Extract only the columns needed for the clustering process. The
iloc method of pandas DataFrame allows for
# integer-location based indexing / selection by position. Here, we
are selecting all rows and all columns
# from the third column onwards.
X = df.iloc[:, 2:]


# Initialize a KMeans model with the number of clusters set to 3.
This means the algorithm will aim to find
# 3 clusters in our data.
model = KMeans(n_clusters=3)


# Train the KMeans model on our dataset. The fit method calculates
the centroids of the 3 clusters and the
# distances from each data point to each centroid.
model.fit(X)


# Obtain the labels of each data point (which cluster it belongs
to) after training.
clusters = model.labels_


# Add a new column 'cluster' to the DataFrame, which holds the
cluster labels for each data point.
# This allows us to know which cluster each data point was
assigned to.
X = X.assign(cluster=clusters)


# Use the sample method of pandas DataFrame to randomly select 10
rows from our dataset, which now includes
# the assigned cluster labels, giving us a quick snapshot of our
clustered data.
X.sample(10)
```

PYTHON OUTPUT

	Age	Annual Income (k$)	Spending Score (1-100)	cluster
51	33	42	60	0
192	33	113	8	2
13	24	20	77	0
37	30	34	73	0
103	26	62	55	0
106	66	63	50	0
114	18	65	48	0
72	60	50	49	0
70	70	49	55	0
19	35	23	98	0

8. Visualize the clusters using scatter plots and a 3D visualization:

PYTHON CODE

```
import plotly.express as px

fig = px.scatter_3d(X, x='Age', y='Annual Income (k$)', z='Spending
Score (1-100)', color='cluster', opacity=0.7)

# Adjusting layout for better visualization
fig.update_layout(margin=dict(l=0, r=0, b=0, t=0))
```

PYTHON OUTPUT

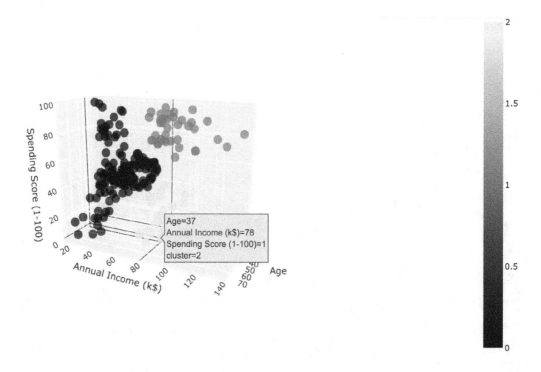

9. Discuss the interpretation of the clustering results and analyze customer behaviors based on the clusters obtained.

10. Summarize the key concepts covered in the lesson, allowing time for students to ask questions and clarify any doubts they may have.

LESSON 16.
STUDY OF PREDICTIVE MODELING WITH MOBILE PRICES DATASET

Lesson Objectives:

This lesson aims to introduce students to the applications of the Pandas library in data manipulation and analysis, with a focus on predictive modeling using Random Forest Classifier. By the end of the lesson, students will learn to import and analyze data using Pandas, prepare the data for machine learning, apply a Random Forest Classifier for predictive modeling, and compare it with other classifiers. The overarching goal is to foster a strong understanding of data manipulation and transformation with Pandas and harnessing the power of machine learning for practical tasks.

Lesson Plan:

I. Introduction to Mobile Prices Dataset

A. Briefly describe the dataset and its features

B. Explain the task of predicting mobile prices based on the given features

II. Baseline Solution with Random Forest Classifier

A. Import the necessary libraries and load the dataset

B. Set the target variable and features

C. Split the data into training and validation sets

D. Create the classifier and fit it to the training data

E. Predict classes using the validation features

F. Calculate the accuracy as the performance metric

G. Discuss the baseline solution and its accuracy

III. Exploring Other Classifiers

A. Introduce additional classifiers: SVC, K-Nearest Neighbors, Decision Tree

B. Train and evaluate each classifier using the same training and validation sets

C. Compare the accuracy of each classifier

D. Discuss the pros and cons of different classifiers

IV. Selecting the Best Classifier

A. Compare the accuracy of different classifiers

B. Consider other factors such as computational complexity, interpretability, and suitability for the task

C. Select the best classifier based on performance and other relevant criteria

V. Conclusion and Discussion

A. Summarize the key points covered in the lesson

B. Discuss the importance of evaluating different classifiers

C. Encourage further exploration and experimentation with other machine learning algorithms

D. Answer any questions and facilitate a discussion on the topic

Lesson Description:

The lesson commences with the exploration of a mobile prices dataset. Students will learn about the features of this dataset and the task of predicting mobile prices. This serves as a real-world example of how Python's

Pandas library and machine learning can be utilized for valuable insights.

We then delve into the creation of a baseline solution using the Random Forest Classifier from the sklearn library. Random Forest is an ensemble learning method that operates by constructing multiple decision trees at training time and outputting the class that is the mode of the classes (classification) or mean prediction (regression) of the individual trees. It effectively reduces overfitting by averaging the results from different trees and provides a way of measuring feature importance.

After loading the dataset using the `read_csv()` function from Pandas, we specify the target variable and features. Using the sklearn's `train_test_split()`, we split the data into training and validation sets. The next step is creating the classifier using `RandomForestClassifier()` and fitting it to the training data with the `fit()` method. We predict classes using the validation features with the `predict()` method, and then calculate the accuracy of the model as the performance metric using sklearn's `accuracy_score()`. The baseline solution and its accuracy are then discussed to set a point of reference for other classifiers.

The lesson progresses by introducing other classifiers: Support Vector Classifier (SVC), K-Nearest Neighbors (KNN), and Decision Tree. Each of these classifiers will be trained and evaluated using the same training and validation sets as the Random Forest Classifier. The accuracy of each classifier is compared, and their pros and cons are discussed to give students an idea of the trade-offs involved in machine learning model selection.

Choosing the best classifier is a critical step in machine learning, and students will learn to do this based on performance and other relevant criteria. They will understand the importance of considering factors such as computational complexity, interpretability, and suitability for the task.

The lesson concludes by summarizing the key points covered, including data manipulation using Pandas, predictive modeling using Random Forest Classifier, and comparison of different classifiers. Students will be encouraged to experiment with other machine learning algorithms and datasets. A Q&A session will be held to address any questions and facilitate a discussion on the topic.

Detailed Lesson Notes:

I. Introduction to Mobile Prices Dataset

1. Briefly describe the Mobile Prices Dataset, including the available features and the task of predicting mobile prices. Download from Kaggle web site[1] train.csv and rename it to Mobile_Prices.csv.

2. Explain the importance of understanding the dataset and its features before applying machine learning algorithms.

II. Baseline Solution with Random Forest Classifier

1. Import the necessary libraries and load the dataset:

PYTHON CODE

```python
import pandas as pd
from sklearn.model_selection import train_test_split
from sklearn.ensemble import RandomForestClassifier
import sklearn.metrics as metrics

data = pd.read_csv('Mobile_Prices.csv')
```

---

1 https://www.kaggle.com/datasets/iabhishekofficial/mobile-price-classification?select=train.csv

2. Set the target variable and features:

```python
y = data['price_range']
X = data.drop('price_range', axis=1)
```

3. Split the data into training and validation sets:

```python
train_X, val_X, train_y, val_y = train_test_split(X, y,
random_state=7)
```

4. Create the classifier and fit it to the training data:

```python
model = RandomForestClassifier(random_state=7, n_estimators=100)
model.fit(train_X, train_y)
```

```
RandomForestClassifier
RandomForestClassifier(random_state=7)
```

5. Predict classes using the validation features:

PYTHON CODE

```python
pred_y = model.predict(val_X)
```

6. Calculate the accuracy as the performance metric:

PYTHON CODE

```python
accuracy = metrics.accuracy_score(val_y, pred_y)
print("Accuracy: ", accuracy)
```

PYTHON OUTPUT

```
Accuracy: 0.864
```

7. Discuss the baseline solution and its accuracy, emphasizing the need for further exploration and improvement.

III. Exploring Other Classifiers

1. Introduce additional classifiers: SVC, K-Nearest Neighbors, Decision Tree.
2. Train and evaluate each classifier using the same training and validation sets:

PYTHON CODE

```python
# Import relevant machine learning models from the scikit-
learn library.
# The Support Vector Classifier (SVC), RandomForestClassifier,
KNeighborsClassifier and DecisionTreeClassifier
# are all different algorithms used for classification tasks.
from sklearn.svm import SVC
from sklearn.neighbors import KNeighborsClassifier
from sklearn.tree import DecisionTreeClassifier

# Create a list containing instances of each classifier. These will
be our models to train and evaluate.
classifiers = [SVC(), RandomForestClassifier(),
KNeighborsClassifier(), DecisionTreeClassifier()]

# Iterate through each classifier in the list
for classifier in classifiers:

    # Train the current classifier with the training data.
    The fit method takes two parameters:
    # the features (train_X) and the corresponding
    labels (train_y).
    classifier.fit(train_X, train_y)

    # Once the model has been trained, use it to predict
    the labels of the validation data.
    pred_y = classifier.predict(val_X)

    # Calculate the accuracy of the predictions. Accuracy is
    the ratio of correct predictions
    # to total predictions. We use the accuracy_score function
    from sklearn's metrics module.
```

```
accuracy = metrics.accuracy_score(val_y, pred_y)

# Print the class name of the classifier and its
accuracy score.
# The class's name is accessed with __class__.__name__,
a built-in attribute in Python.
print(classifier.__class__.__name__, "Accuracy:", accuracy)
```

PYTHON OUTPUT

```
SVC Accuracy: 0.956
RandomForestClassifier Accuracy: 0.87
KNeighborsClassifier Accuracy: 0.926
DecisionTreeClassifier Accuracy: 0.814
```

---

3. Compare the accuracy of each classifier and discuss their pros and cons, considering factors such as computational complexity, interpretability, and suitability for the task.

IV. Selecting the Best Classifier

1. Compare the accuracy of different classifiers and consider other factors:
   - Computational complexity: How computationally expensive is the model?
   - Interpretability: How easy is it to interpret the model's decisions?

- Suitability for the task: Does the classifier's characteristics align with the problem requirements?
2. Select the best classifier based on performance and other relevant criteria.

V. Conclusion and Discussion

1. Summarize the key points covered in the lesson, including the baseline solution, exploring different classifiers, and selecting the best classifier.
2. Discuss the importance of comparing and evaluating different classifiers for a specific machine learning problem.
3. Encourage further exploration and experimentation with other machine learning algorithms.
4. Answer any questions and facilitate a discussion on the topic.

Note:

Ensure to provide appropriate explanations, code annotations, and address any questions or concerns from the students during the lesson.

LESSON 17.
CORRELATIONS, METRICS, AND PREDICTING OUTCOME

Lesson Objectives:

This lesson is intended to provide learners with an understanding of advanced concepts in machine learning, including the determination of feature importance with a Random Forest Classifier, measuring linear correlation with Pearson's coefficient, and analyzing model performance using a confusion matrix. At the end of the lesson, learners will be proficient in understanding and calculating feature importance, correlating features, and interpreting confusion matrices. The goal is to enable students to delve deeper into machine learning concepts and metrics, thus enhancing their predictive modeling skills.

Lesson Plan:

I. Feature Importance in Random Forest Classifier

A. Understanding the concept of feature importance

B. Using the Random Forest Classifier to determine feature importance

C. Analyzing and interpreting the results

II. Correlations and Pearson's Correlation Coefficient

A. Explaining the concept of correlation

B. Using Pearson's correlation coefficient to measure linear correlation

C. Visualizing correlations using a heatmap

III. False Positive and False Negative: Confusion Matrix

A. Introduction to the confusion matrix

B. Understanding false positive and false negative rates

C. Calculating and interpreting the confusion matrix

IV. Review and Q&A

A. Reviewing the day's lesson

B. Time for questions and answers

Lesson Description:

The lesson starts with an exploration of feature importance in the context of a Random Forest Classifier. Feature importance is a powerful concept that allows us to understand which features are most influential in making predictions. Using the sklearn's `RandomForestClassifier` and its `feature_importances_` attribute, we'll see how we can quantify the significance of each feature in our dataset. The interpretation of these values and their implications for model building will be thoroughly explained.

Next, we transition to the concept of correlation and the use of Pearson's correlation coefficient to measure linear correlation between features. The students will learn about the `corr()` method from Pandas, which computes pairwise correlation of columns, excluding NA/null values. To visualize these correlations, the seaborn library's `heatmap()` function will be used, providing an intuitive, color-coded representation of the data.

Following this, we turn our attention to understanding model performance beyond accuracy, through the concept of a confusion matrix. Here, we introduce the terms true positive, true negative, false positive, and false negative. These concepts help us understand the type of errors our model is making. We will use the `confusion_matrix()` function from sklearn to calculate the confusion matrix. Understanding these metrics enables more nuanced assessment of model performance, particularly in scenarios where prediction errors have varying consequences.

The lesson concludes with a comprehensive review of the day's topics, from feature importance in a Random Forest Classifier to correlation measurement with Pearson's coefficient, and understanding model performance through a confusion matrix. A Q&A session will provide students with the opportunity to clarify any questions or doubts about these advanced machine learning concepts. In the end, students are encouraged to explore these topics further and apply these techniques to their datasets.

Detailed Lesson Notes:

1. Start by explaining the concept of feature importance. Feature importance represents the contribution of each feature in a machine learning model towards making accurate predictions.

2. Introduce the Random Forest Classifier as a machine learning model used for feature importance analysis. Explain that it can rank features based on their importance scores.

3. Demonstrate how to calculate and interpret feature importance using a Random Forest Classifier. Use the following code:

PYTHON CODE

```
# Import the necessary libraries: pandas for data manipulation,
numpy for numerical computations,
# and the relevant parts of sklearn for model creation
and training.
import pandas as pd
import numpy as np
from sklearn.model_selection import train_test_split
from sklearn.ensemble import RandomForestClassifier

# Load the dataset 'Mobile_Prices.csv' using pandas' read_csv
function into a DataFrame named 'data'.
data = pd.read_csv('Mobile_Prices.csv')

# Create the target vector 'y' that the model will learn to
predict, which is the 'price_range' column in the dataset.
y = data['price_range']

# Create the feature matrix 'X' by dropping the 'price_range'
column from the original dataset.
```

```python
# This leaves us with a DataFrame where each column is a feature
# and each row is a data point.
X = data.drop('price_range', axis=1)

# Split the dataset into a training set and a validation set using
# sklearn's train_test_split function.
# The 'random_state' parameter is set to ensure that the splits
# you generate are reproducible.
train_X, val_X, train_y, val_y = train_test_split(X, y,
random_state=7)

# Initialize a RandomForestClassifier object. This is a type of
# machine learning model that uses an ensemble of decision trees.
# 'random_state' is set for reproducibility, 'n_estimators' denotes
# the number of trees in the forest.
model = RandomForestClassifier(random_state=7, n_estimators=100)

# Train the RandomForest model on the training data.
model.fit(train_X, train_y)

# Extract feature importance from the trained RandomForest model.
# These importances are then rounded to three decimal places.
# This is then converted into a DataFrame for easier visualization
# and handling.
importances = pd.DataFrame({'feature': train_X.columns,
'importance': np.round(model.feature_importances_, 3)})
# Sort the importances DataFrame by the 'importance' column in
# descending order and set 'feature' as the index.
importances = importances.sort_values('importance',
ascending=False).set_index('feature')
```

```
# Display the top 15 features as per their importance
in the model.
print(importances.head(15))
```

PYTHON OUTPUT

	importance
feature	
ram	0.477
battery_power	0.077
px_width	0.059
px_height	0.056
mobile_wt	0.039
int_memory	0.038
talk_time	0.029
sc_w	0.029
pc	0.029
clock_speed	0.029
sc_h	0.027
m_dep	0.025
fc	0.024
n_cores	0.023
blue	0.007

4. Discuss the concept of correlations and how they measure the linear relationship between two sets of data.

5. Introduce Pearson's correlation coefficient as a measure of linear correlation. Explain that it ranges from -1 to 1, where -1 indicates a strong negative correlation,

0 indicates no correlation, and 1 indicates a strong positive correlation.

6. Show how to calculate and visualize correlations using Pearson's correlation coefficient. Use the following code:

PYTHON CODE

```python
import seaborn as sns
import matplotlib.pyplot as plt
# Calculate the correlation matrix
correlation_matrix = train_X.corr()

# Round the correlation matrix to 1 digits after the decimal
rounded_corr_matrix = correlation_matrix.round(2)

# Print the rounded correlation matrix
print(rounded_corr_matrix)

#Display the heatmap
sns.heatmap(correlation_matrix, vmin=-1, vmax=1, annot=False,
cmap='BrBG')
plt.show()
```

PYTHON OUTPUT

	battery_power	blue	clock_speed	dual_sim	fc	four_g \
battery_power	1.00	-0.00	0.00	-0.04	0.03	0.00
blue	-0.00	1.00	0.01	0.04	0.00	0.01
clock_speed	0.00	0.01	1.00	-0.03	0.01	-0.02
dual_sim	-0.04	0.04	-0.03	1.00	-0.02	0.01

fc	0.03	0.00	0.01	-0.02	1.00	-0.03
four_g	0.00	0.01	-0.02	0.01	-0.03	1.00
int_memory	-0.03	0.06	-0.02	-0.04	-0.02	0.03
m_dep	0.04	0.01	0.02	-0.04	0.02	0.01
mobile_wt	0.01	-0.00	0.02	0.01	-0.00	-0.02
n_cores	-0.06	0.04	-0.02	-0.03	-0.00	-0.02
pc	0.04	-0.00	0.02	-0.01	0.64	-0.01
px_height	-0.01	-0.00	-0.03	0.00	-0.01	-0.02
px_width	-0.01	-0.03	-0.03	0.02	-0.01	0.02
ram	-0.02	0.02	-0.00	0.03	-0.01	0.01
sc_h	-0.05	-0.00	-0.06	-0.02	-0.02	0.02
sc_w	-0.03	-0.00	-0.03	-0.01	-0.01	0.06
talk_time	0.07	0.02	-0.01	-0.05	0.01	-0.05
three_g	-0.01	-0.04	-0.04	0.00	-0.01	0.58
touch_screen	-0.02	0.02	0.02	-0.00	-0.01	0.03
wifi	-0.02	-0.02	-0.03	0.01	-0.00	-0.02

	int_memory	m_dep	mobile_wt	n_cores	pc	px_height \
battery_power	-0.03	0.04	0.01	-0.06	0.04	-0.01
blue	0.06	0.01	-0.00	0.04	-0.00	-0.00
clock_speed	-0.02	0.02	0.02	-0.02	0.02	-0.03
dual_sim	-0.04	-0.04	0.01	-0.03	-0.01	0.00
fc	-0.02	0.02	-0.00	-0.00	0.64	-0.01
four_g	0.03	0.01	-0.02	-0.02	-0.01	-0.02
int_memory	1.00	-0.00	-0.04	-0.02	-0.04	0.01
m_dep	-0.00	1.00	0.03	0.02	0.03	0.05
mobile_wt	-0.04	0.03	1.00	-0.03	0.02	0.00
n_cores	-0.02	0.02	-0.03	1.00	0.00	-0.02
pc	-0.04	0.03	0.02	0.00	1.00	-0.03
px_height	0.01	0.05	0.00	-0.02	-0.03	1.00
px_width	-0.01	0.05	-0.01	0.02	0.00	0.51
ram	0.04	-0.02	-0.00	0.01	0.01	-0.02
sc_h	0.04	-0.02	-0.04	-0.02	-0.01	0.06
sc_w	0.04	-0.01	-0.02	0.02	-0.02	0.04
talk_time	0.01	0.04	0.02	0.03	0.03	-0.03

three_g	-0.00	-0.01	-0.00	-0.02	0.01	-0.02
touch_screen	-0.01	-0.00	-0.02	0.04	-0.01	0.01
wifi	0.02	-0.02	-0.01	0.01	-0.01	0.06

	px_width	ram	sc_h	sc_w	talk_time	three_g	touch_screen \
battery_power	-0.01	-0.02	-0.05	-0.03	0.07	-0.01	-0.02
blue	-0.03	0.02	-0.00	-0.00	0.02	-0.04	0.02
clock_speed	-0.03	-0.00	-0.06	-0.03	-0.01	-0.04	0.02
dual_sim	0.02	0.03	-0.02	-0.01	-0.05	0.00	-0.00
fc	-0.01	-0.01	-0.02	-0.01	0.01	-0.01	-0.01
four_g	0.02	0.01	0.02	0.06	-0.05	0.58	0.03
int_memory	-0.01	0.04	0.04	0.04	0.01	-0.00	-0.01
m_dep	0.05	-0.02	-0.02	-0.01	0.04	-0.01	-0.00
mobile_wt	-0.01	-0.00	-0.04	-0.02	0.02	-0.00	-0.02
n_cores	0.02	0.01	-0.02	0.02	0.03	-0.02	0.04
pc	0.00	0.01	-0.01	-0.02	0.03	0.01	-0.01
px_height	0.51	-0.02	0.06	0.04	-0.03	-0.02	0.01
px_width	1.00	-0.01	0.01	0.02	0.02	0.01	-0.02
ram	-0.01	1.00	0.02	0.02	0.03	0.00	-0.03
sc_h	0.01	0.02	1.00	0.51	-0.05	0.01	-0.02
sc_w	0.02	0.02	0.51	1.00	-0.04	0.05	0.01
talk_time	0.02	0.03	-0.05	-0.04	1.00	-0.05	0.01
three_g	0.01	0.00	0.01	0.05	-0.05	1.00	0.04
touch_screen	-0.02	-0.03	-0.02	0.01	0.01	0.04	1.00
wifi	0.05	0.02	0.02	0.04	-0.05	-0.01	0.01

	wifi
battery_power	-0.02
blue	-0.02
clock_speed	-0.03
dual_sim	0.01
fc	-0.00
four_g	-0.02
int_memory	0.02
m_dep	-0.02
mobile_wt	-0.01
n_cores	0.01

pc	-0.01
px_height	0.06
px_width	0.05
ram	0.02
sc_h	0.02
sc_w	0.04
talk_time	-0.05
three_g	-0.01
touch_screen	0.01
wifi	1.00

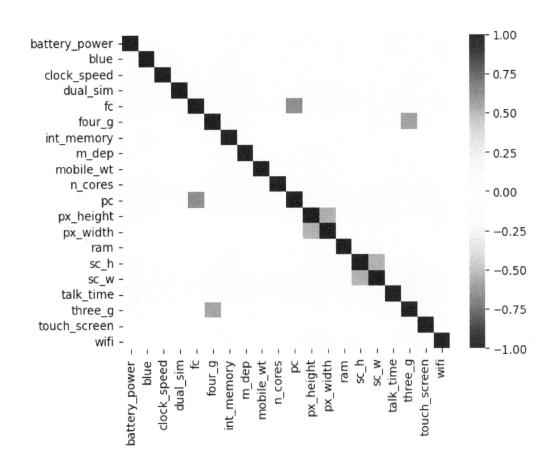

7. Explain the concept of false positive and false negative rates in the context of binary classification problems.

8. Introduce the confusion matrix as a tool to evaluate predictions and calculate false positive and false negative rates.

9. Demonstrate how to calculate and interpret the confusion matrix. Use the following code:

PYTHON CODE

```python
# Import the confusion_matrix function from the sklearn.
metrics module.
# This function computes the confusion matrix, which is a summary
of prediction results on a classification problem.
from sklearn.metrics import confusion_matrix

# Use the predict method of the model to make predictions on the
validation data. The model is presumably a
# machine learning model that has been trained already. val_X is
the feature data for the validation set.
pred_y = model.predict(val_X)

# Compute the confusion matrix. val_y is the true target values
for the validation set, and pred_y is the predicted
# target values that we just computed. The confusion_matrix
function compares each predicted value to the true
# value and increments the count in the appropriate cell of the
confusion matrix.
confusion_matrix(val_y, pred_y)
```

PYTHON OUTPUT

```
array([[130,    6,    0,    0],
       [  4,   91,   15,    0],
       [  0,   21,   98,   12],
       [  0,    0,   10,  113]])
```

10. Summarize the key concepts of the lesson, allowing
    time for students to ask questions and clarifying
    any doubts they may have.

LESSON 18.
LEARNING FROM THE
TITANIC DISASTER

Lesson Objectives:

The goal of this lesson is to familiarize students with a real-world application of the Random Forest Classifier in Python, namely predicting survival on the Titanic. Learners will be exposed to various aspects of the data science pipeline including data loading and inspection, exploratory data analysis, model creation, and prediction output. By the end of this lesson, students should be comfortable with implementing a Random Forest Classifier and interpreting its results, setting the stage for further exploration of machine learning algorithms.

Lesson Plan:

I. Introduction and Data Loading

A. Importing the necessary libraries: numpy, pandas, RandomForestClassifier

B. Loading the train.csv and test.csv datasets

C. Checking the loaded data: shape, missing values, and data types

II. Gender-Based Survival Analysis

A. Analyzing the survival rates for men and women

B. Calculating the percentage of women and men who survived

III. Creating a Predictive Model using Random Forest Classifier

A. Explaining the Random Forest Classifier algorithm

B. Defining the target variable y as "Survived"

C. Selecting the features to be used in the model

D. Preparing the feature matrix X using one-hot encoding with pd.get_dummies()

E. Training the Random Forest Classifier model using the fit() method

F. Making predictions using the trained model on the test dataset

IV. Outputting the Predictions

    A. Creating an output DataFrame with the PassengerId and predicted Survived values

    B. Displaying the output DataFrame

V. Next Steps and Discussion

    A. Introduction to accuracy evaluation and ways to improve the prediction

    B. Briefly outline the topics to be covered in the next lesson

Lesson Description:

Our lesson begins with the necessary setup and data loading. We import crucial libraries like numpy and pandas for data handling, and RandomForestClassifier from sklearn.ensemble for our machine learning model. Subsequently, the 'train.csv' and 'test.csv' datasets are loaded using pandas' `read_csv()` function. Students will learn about initial data exploration methods such as checking the shape of the dataset, detecting missing values, and identifying data types using pandas methods like `shape`, `isnull().sum()`, and `info()`.

Next, we dive into some exploratory data analysis, examining survival rates on the Titanic by gender. The `groupby()` and `mean()` functions from pandas will be utilized to calculate the survival percentages for both men and women. This will showcase how pandas can be leveraged for quick and easy statistical analysis.

Once our data understanding is established, we move to the creation of a Random Forest Classifier predictive model. The RandomForestClassifier algorithm, part of the sklearn.ensemble module, is introduced and explained. We define our target variable 'y' to be 'Survived' and select our model's features. Students will gain exposure to one-hot encoding via the pandas' `get_dummies()` function to prepare the feature matrix 'X'. This encoding technique transforms categorical variables into a format that works better with classification algorithms. We then fit our model to the training data using the `fit()` method from RandomForestClassifier and make predictions on the test dataset.

Upon obtaining our model's predictions, we create an output DataFrame containing 'PassengerId' and the predicted 'Survived' values. The resulting DataFrame is displayed to the students using the `head()` function, showcasing the predicted survival outcome for passengers.

In the final segment of the lesson, we discuss possible next steps, including model accuracy evaluation and potential improvements. We will then outline what to expect in the next lesson, encouraging students to continue exploring and learning. This lesson sets the foundation for more advanced machine learning concepts and techniques in the future.

Detailed Lesson Notes:

I.   Introduction and Data Loading

1. Import the necessary libraries and explain their purposes:

PYTHON CODE

```python
# Import the numpy library, a fundamental package for scientific
computing with Python. It provides support for arrays, along with
a collection of mathematical functions to operate on these arrays.
import numpy as np

# Import the pandas library, a powerful data manipulation and
analysis tool. It offers data structures and operations for
```

manipulating numerical tables and time-series data. It's built on top of two core Python libraries – Matplotlib for data visualization and NumPy for mathematical operations.

```python
import pandas as pd
```

```python
# Import the RandomForestClassifier class from the sklearn.
# ensemble module. This is a meta-estimator that fits a number of
# decision tree classifiers on various sub-samples of the dataset
# and uses averaging to improve the predictive accuracy and control
# overfitting. It's a popular choice for classification tasks.
from sklearn.ensemble import RandomForestClassifier
```

---

2. Download Titanic test and train datasets from Kaggle website[1]. We partitioned the data into two sets: training and testing. The training portion educates the machine on making predictions, while the testing portion assesses the proficiency of its learning. Load the train.csv and test.csv datasets:

PYTHON CODE

```python
# Load the training data set into a pandas DataFrame. The function
# pd.read_csv() is a pandas function that reads a CSV file and
# converts it into a DataFrame. The file "train.csv" is assumed to be
# in the same directory as this script. If it were in # a different
# directory, you'd need to specify the full path to the file.
```

---

1 https://www.kaggle.com/competitions/titanic/data

```
train_data = pd.read_csv("train.csv")
```

```
# Similarly, load the testing data set into a pandas DataFrame.
The data in "test.csv" is separate from the training data and will
be used to evaluate the performance of a machine learning model
trained on 'train_data'. Like with the training data, this file is
assumed to be in the same directory as the script.
test_data = pd.read_csv("test.csv")
```

---

3. Check the loaded data: shape, missing values, and data types:

PYTHON CODE

```
# The 'shape' attribute of a pandas DataFrame gives the
dimensions of the DataFrame. It returns a tuple representing the
dimensionality of the DataFrame where the first element is the
number of rows and the second element is the number of columns.
Here, we're printing the shape of both the train and test datasets
to get a sense of their size.
print(train_data.shape, test_data.shape)
```

```
# The 'isnull()' function returns a DataFrame where each cell
is either True or False depending on whether that cell's value
is null or not. The 'sum()' function then sums these boolean
values column-wise (True is treated as 1 and False as 0),
giving the total number of null values in each column. 'sort_
values(ascending=False)' then sorts these values in descending
order. This is a useful way of quickly identifying columns with
missing values in the training dataset.
```

```
print("Train data:\n", train_data.isnull().sum().sort_
values(ascending=False))
print("Test data:\n",test_data.isnull().sum().sort_
values(ascending=False))

# The 'dtypes' attribute returns a Series with the data type
of each column. The result's index is the original DataFrame's
columns. This gives us a quick overview of the kind of data in
each column - whether they're integers, floats, objects (possibly
strings), etc.
train_data.dtypes
```

PYTHON OUTPUT

```
(891, 12) (418, 11)
Train data:
 Cabin          687
Age            177
Embarked         2
PassengerId      0
Survived         0
Pclass           0
Name             0
Sex              0
SibSp            0
Parch            0
Ticket           0
Fare             0
dtype: int64
Test data:
 Cabin          327
Age             86
Fare             1
```

```
PassengerId    0
Pclass         0
Name           0
Sex            0
SibSp          0
Parch          0
Ticket         0
Embarked       0
dtype: int64
PassengerId    int64
Survived       int64
Pclass         int64
Name           object
Sex            object
Age            float64
SibSp          int64
Parch          int64
Ticket         object
Fare           float64
Cabin          object
Embarked       object
dtype: object
```

II. Gender-Based Survival Analysis

1. Analyze the survival rates for men and women and
   explain the calculations:

PYTHON CODE

```
# Extract the 'Survived' column values from the training data
where the 'Sex' column is 'female'.
# We use the 'loc' function, which is primarily label based
indexing. It is used with a boolean array, and it returns a
DataFrame consisting of rows where 'Sex' is 'female'. From these
rows, we only keep the 'Survived' column.
# This 'Survived' data for female passengers is then stored in the
'women' variable.
women = train_data.loc[train_data.Sex == 'female']["Survived"]


# Calculate the survival rate of women by taking the sum of
the 'women' series (since 'Survived' is a binary column with 1
representing survival) and dividing by the total number of women.
This gives us the proportion of women who survived.
rate_women = round(sum(women) / len(women),2)


# Print the survival rate of women in the training data.
print("Percentage of women who survived:", rate_women)


# Similarly, extract the 'Survived' column values for
male passengers.
men = train_data.loc[train_data.Sex == 'male']["Survived"]


# Calculate the survival rate of men in a similar fashion to the
women's survival rate calculation.
rate_men = round(sum(men) / len(men), 2)


# Print the survival rate of men in the training data.
print("Percentage of men who survived:", rate_men)
```

PYTHON OUTPUT

```
Percentage of women who survived: 0.74
Percentage of men who survived: 0.19
```

III. Creating a Predictive Model using Random Forest Classifier

1. Explain the Random Forest Classifier algorithm:
   - Random Forest is an ensemble learning method that combines multiple decision trees to make predictions.
   - It randomly selects a subset of features and builds multiple decision trees using different subsets of the data.
   - The predictions from each tree are combined to make the final prediction.
2. Define the target variable y as "Survived":

PYTHON CODE

```
y = train_data["Survived"]
```

3. Select the features to be used in the model and explain their significance:

PYTHON CODE

```python
features = ["Pclass", "Sex", "SibSp", "Parch"]
```

4. Prepare the feature matrix X using one-hot encoding with pd.get_dummies():

PYTHON CODE

```python
X = pd.get_dummies(train_data[features])
```

5. Train the Random Forest Classifier model using the fit() method:

PYTHON CODE

```python
model = RandomForestClassifier(n_estimators=100, max_depth=5,
random_state=1)
model.fit(X, y)
```

PYTHON OUTPUT

```
RandomForestClassifier
RandomForestClassifier(max_depth=5, random_state=1)
```

6. Make predictions using the trained model on the test dataset:

PYTHON CODE

```python
X_test = pd.get_dummies(test_data[features])
predictions = model.predict(X_test)
```

IV. Outputting the Predictions

1. Create an output DataFrame with the PassengerId and predicted Survived values:

PYTHON CODE

```python
output = pd.DataFrame({'PassengerId': test_data.PassengerId,
'Survived': predictions})
```

2. Display the output DataFrame:

PYTHON CODE

```python
print(output)
```

PYTHON OUTPUT

```
     PassengerId   Survived
0            892          0
1            893          1
2            894          0
3            895          0
4            896          1
..           ...        ...
```

```
413          1305          0
414          1306          1
415          1307          0
416          1308          0
417          1309          0

[418 rows x 2 columns]
```

V.   Next Steps and Discussion

1. Introduce the concept of accuracy evaluation and ways to improve the prediction.
2. Briefly outline the topics to be covered in the next lesson.

LESSON 19.
MEASURING AND IMPROVING MODEL ACCURACY

Lesson Objectives:

The goal of this lesson is to provide students with a comprehensive understanding of how to preprocess datasets, create and evaluate multiple machine learning models using Python. The primary focus will be on demonstrating the utility of train-test split, handling missing values, scaling features, and evaluating model accuracy. By the end of the lesson, students will be familiar with the fundamental steps of a machine learning project and be capable of implementing, comparing, and discussing the results of various classifiers.

Lesson Plan:

I.   Introduction and Data Loading

    A. Importing the necessary libraries: numpy, pandas, sklearn.ensemble.RandomForestClassifier, sklearn.svm.SVC, sklearn.linear_model.LogisticRegression, sklearn.neighbors.KNeighborsClassifier, sklearn.tree.DecisionTreeClassifier, sklearn.model_selection.train_test_split, sklearn.preprocessing.MinMaxScaler, sklearn.preprocessing.LabelEncoder

    B. Loading the train.csv and test.csv datasets

    C. Checking the loaded data: shape, missing values, and data types

    D. Explaining the purpose of train-test split and its benefits

II. Data Preprocessing and Train-Test Split

    A. Handling missing values by dropping rows with missing values in the "Embarked" and "Fare" columns

III. Creating and Evaluating Multiple Models

    A. Introduction to model accuracy and evaluation metrics

    B. Selecting the features to be used in the models

    C. Preprocessing the data using MinMaxScaler

    D. Training and evaluating the following models:

1. Random Forest Classifier
2. K-Nearest Neighbors Classifier
3. Support Vector Classifier
4. Logistic Regression
5. Decision Tree Classifier

E. Comparing and discussing the accuracy scores of the models

IV. Next Steps and Discussion

A. Summary of the lesson and key takeaways
B. Discussion on potential ways to improve model accuracy

Lesson Description:

The lesson starts by introducing and importing all necessary libraries and modules. We will be using numpy and pandas for data manipulation, RandomForestClassifier, SVC, LogisticRegression, KNeighborsClassifier, DecisionTreeClassifier from sklearn for creating our models, and train_test_split, MinMaxScaler, LabelEncoder from sklearn for preprocessing and splitting our data. The 'train.csv' and 'test.csv' datasets will be loaded using the `read_csv()` function from pandas. Next, we examine the datasets using methods like `shape`, `isnull().

sum()`, and `info()` to understand the structure, identify missing values, and recognize the data types. We will also delve into the concept of train-test split, discussing its significance in model evaluation and preventing overfitting.

In the data preprocessing segment, we handle missing values in the "Embarked" and "Fare" columns by dropping rows with `dropna()`. This is a basic technique for dealing with missing data, which students will find crucial in real-world data cleaning tasks.

The lesson then moves to the main task of creating and evaluating multiple models. The concept of model accuracy and various evaluation metrics are explained. After feature selection, we introduce the MinMaxScaler from sklearn's preprocessing module, which transforms features by scaling each feature to a given range, helping to improve the performance of our models. We train and evaluate five different models: Random Forest Classifier, K-Neighbors Classifier, Support Vector Classifier, Logistic Regression, and Decision Tree Classifier. The fit() and score() methods are utilized for training the models and assessing their performance.

In the final part of the lesson, we compare the accuracy scores of the models, fostering a discussion on their strengths and weaknesses. The summary of the lesson and key takeaways are discussed, with a focus on how to improve model accuracy, thus motivating students to further explore the depth of machine learning.

Detailed Lesson Notes:

I.   Introduction and Data Loading

1. Import the necessary libraries and explain their purposes:

PYTHON CODE

```python
# Import the 'numpy' library which provides functionality for
handling arrays and applying mathematical operations on them, it's
fundamental to scientific computation with Python.
import numpy as np

# Import 'pandas', a versatile data manipulation library in Python
that provides flexible data structures and data analysis tools.
import pandas as pd
# Import the 'RandomForestClassifier' from the 'sklearn.ensemble'
module. A Random Forest is an ensemble machine learning technique
that constructs multiple decision trees and merges them together
to obtain a more accurate and stable prediction.
```

```python
from sklearn.ensemble import RandomForestClassifier

# Import the 'SVC' (Support Vector Classifier) from the 'sklearn.
svm' module. The SVC is a machine learning model that is
often used for classification tasks, especially in high
dimensional spaces.
from sklearn.svm import SVC

# Import the 'LogisticRegression' class from the 'sklearn.linear_
model' module. Logistic regression is a statistical model used in
binary classification where the output is a probability that the#
given input point belongs to a certain class.
from sklearn.linear_model import LogisticRegression

# Import the 'KNeighborsClassifier' from the 'sklearn.neighbors'
module. This is a type of instance-based learning or non-
generalizing learning where the function is only approximated
locally and all computation is deferred until classification.
from sklearn.neighbors import KNeighborsClassifier

# Import the 'DecisionTreeClassifier' from the 'sklearn.tree'
module. Decision trees are a type of model used in data mining
for deriving a strategy to reach a specific goal, its also a common
model for machine learning.
from sklearn.tree import DecisionTreeClassifier
# Import the 'MinMaxScaler' from 'sklearn.preprocessing' module.
This estimator scales and translates each feature individually
such that it is in the given range on the training set, i.e
between zero and one.
from sklearn.preprocessing import MinMaxScaler
```

```
# Import 'LabelEncoder' from 'sklearn.preprocessing' module. This
is a utility class to help normalize labels such that they contain
only values between 0 and n_classes-1, often used for encoding
categorical features.
from sklearn.preprocessing import LabelEncoder

# Import 'train_test_split' function from 'sklearn.model_selection'
module which is used to split a dataset into random train and
test subsets.
from sklearn.model_selection import train_test_split
```

---

2. We need to load the 'train.csv' datasets for our analysis. It's important to note that the 'test.csv' dataset, which we utilized in Lesson 12, doesn't include the 'Survived' field. As a result, it isn't suitable for evaluating the performance of different classifiers because it lacks this crucial piece of outcome data.

PYTHON CODE

```
# Load the training data set into a pandas DataFrame. The function
pd.read_csv() is a pandas function that reads a CSV file and
converts it into a DataFrame. The file "train.csv" is assumed to be
in the same directory as this script. If it were in a different
directory, you'd need to specify the full path to the file.
base_dataset = pd.read_csv("train.csv")
```

---

3. Explain the purpose of train-test split and its benefits:
   - Train-test split helps evaluate the model's performance on unseen data.
   - It helps in detecting overfitting or underfitting of the model.
   - It provides an unbiased estimate of the model's performance.

PYTHON CODE

```python
# Data splitting:
# Sampling 80% of the base_dataset for training
# The `sample` method randomly selects a fraction of the data
# The `frac` parameter is set to 0.8, indicating 80% of the dataset
should be selected
# The `random_state` parameter is set to 25 for reproducibility
train_data = base_dataset.sample(frac=0.8, random_state=25)

# Data splitting:
# Creating the test_data by excluding the indices of the train_
data from the base_dataset
# The `drop` method removes rows based on their indices
# The `index` attribute of train_data contains the indices of the
samples selected for training
test_data = base_dataset.drop(train_data.index)
```

---

4. Check the loaded data: shape, missing values, and data types:

PYTHON CODE

```
# The 'shape' attribute of a pandas DataFrame gives the
dimensions of the DataFrame. It returns a tuple representing the
dimensionality of the DataFrame where the first element is the
number of rows and the second element is the number of columns.
Here, we're printing the shape of both the train and test datasets
to get a sense of their size.
print(train_data.shape, test_data.shape)
```

PYTHON OUTPUT

```
(713, 12) (178, 12)
```

PYTHON CODE

```
# The 'isnull()' function returns a DataFrame where each cell
is either True or False depending on whether that cell's value
is null or not. The 'sum()' function then sums these boolean
values column-wise (True is treated as 1 and False as 0),
giving the total number of null values in each column. 'sort_
values(ascending=False)' then sorts these values in descending
order. This is a useful way of quickly identifying columns with
missing values in the training dataset.
print("Train data:\n", train_data.isnull().sum().sort_
values(ascending=False))
print("Test data:\n",test_data.isnull().sum().sort_
values(ascending=False))
```

PYTHON OUTPUT

```
Train data:
 Cabin          548
Age             134
Embarked        1
PassengerId     0
Survived        0
Pclass          0
Name            0
Sex             0
SibSp           0
Parch           0
Ticket          0
Fare            0
dtype: int64
Test data:
 Cabin          139
Age             43
Embarked        1
PassengerId     0
Survived        0
Pclass          0
Name            0
Sex             0
SibSp           0
Parch           0
Ticket          0
Fare            0
dtype: int64
```

PYTHON CODE

```
# The 'dtypes' attribute returns a Series with the data type
of each column. The result's index is the original DataFrame's
columns. This gives us a quick overview of the kind of data in
each column - whether they're integers, floats, objects (possibly
strings), etc.
train_data.dtypes
```

PYTHON OUTPUT

```
PassengerId    int64
Survived       int64
Pclass         int64
Name           object
Sex            object
Age            float64
SibSp          int64
Parch          int64
Ticket         object
Fare           float64
Cabin          object
Embarked       object
dtype: object
```

PYTHON CODE

```
test_data.dtypes
```

PYTHON OUTPUT

```
PassengerId    int64
Survived       int64
```

```
Pclass          int64
Name            object
Sex             object
Age             float64
SibSp           int64
Parch           int64
Ticket          object
Fare            float64
Cabin           object
Embarked        object
dtype: object
```

II. Data Preprocessing

1. Handle missing values by dropping rows with missing values in the "Embarked" and "Fare" columns:

PYTHON CODE

```
# Dropping missing values in train_data and test_data based on
specific columns
# Dropping missing values in train_data:
# The `dropna` method is used to remove rows with missing values
(NaN) in specific columns
# The `subset` parameter is set to ["Embarked", "Fare"], indicating
that rows with missing values in these columns will be dropped
train_data = train_data.dropna(subset=["Embarked", "Fare"])

# Dropping missing values in test_data:
# The same approach is applied to the test_data as in train_data
# The `dropna` method is used to remove rows with missing values
(NaN) in specific columns
```

```python
# The `subset` parameter is set to ["Embarked", "Fare"], indicating
that rows with missing values in these columns will be dropped
test_data = test_data.dropna(subset=["Embarked", "Fare"])
```

III. Creating and Evaluating Multiple Models

1. Introduction to model accuracy and evaluation metrics:
    - Model accuracy measures how well a model predicts the correct outcomes.
    - Evaluation metrics such as accuracy score, precision, recall, and F1-score help assess model performance.
2. Select the features to be used in the models:

PYTHON CODE

```python
# Defining the features to be used in the model

# The variable `features` is being assigned a list of column names
# These columns represent the features that will be used
in the model
features = ["Pclass", "Sex", "SibSp", "Parch", "Fare"]
```

3. Preprocess the data using get_dummies and MinMaxScaler:

PYTHON CODE

```
# Use pandas' 'get_dummies' function on the training data to
convert categorical variable(s) into dummy/indicator variables.
# This process is called one-hot encoding and it creates new
columns for each unique category in the categorical feature(s).
# Each of these new columns will contain 1s and 0s indicating the
presence of that category in the original row.
# The result is stored in 'X_train'.
X_train = pd.get_dummies(train_data[features])


# Repeat the above process for the test data as well, ensuring
that categorical variables in the test data are also converted
into the appropriate number of dummy/indicator variables.
X_test = pd.get_dummies(test_data[features])


# Initialize a 'MinMaxScaler' object, which scales and translates
each feature individually such that it is in the given range on
the training set (between zero and one by default).
scaler = MinMaxScaler()


# Train the scaler using the 'fit' method with 'X_train'. This
calculates the minimum and maximum value of each feature.
scaler.fit(X_train)


# Apply the 'transform' method of the scaler to 'X_train'. This
scales the data based on the min-max values calculated above.
# It adjusts the features of 'X_train' such that they lie between
the range set when we initialized the MinMaxScaler (default: 0-1).
# This transformation is then stored back in 'X_train'.
X_train = scaler.transform(X_train)
# It's important to apply the same scaling to the test data. So,
we fit the scaler on 'X_test' to find the min-max values.
```

```
scaler.fit(X_test)
# Similar to what we did for 'X_train', we now transform 'X_test'
based on these min-max values and store it back into 'X_test'.
X_test = scaler.transform(X_test)
```

---

4. Train and evaluate the Random Forest Classifier model:

PYTHON CODE

```
# We first instantiate a RandomForestClassifier model. The
RandomForestClassifier is a popular machine learning algorithm that
creates a 'forest' of decision trees and outputs the class that
is the mode of the classes of individual trees. In this instance,
we're defining three parameters - 'n_estimators' is set to 100,
indicating we'll have 100 trees in our forest, 'max_depth' is set
to 5, defining the maximum depth of each tree, and 'random_state'
is set to 1, ensuring that our results are reproducible since the
random number generator's seed is set to 1.
model_rf = RandomForestClassifier(n_estimators=100, max_depth=5,
random_state=1)


# We now train the model using the 'fit' method, on our
training data 'X_train' and the corresponding labels 'train_
data["Survived"]'.
model_rf.fit(X_train, train_data["Survived"])
# Then, we evaluate the model's performance on the test data using
the 'score' method, which returns the mean accuracy on the given
test data and labels. The accuracy is then multiplied by 100 to
convert it into percentage and rounded to 2 decimal places using
the 'round' function. The result is stored in 'RF_score'.
```

```
RF_score = round(model_rf.score(X_test, test_
data["Survived"]) * 100, 2)
# Finally, we print out the accuracy of our Random Forest model to
the console.
print("Random Forest:", RF_score)
```

PYTHON OUTPUT

Random Forest: 78.53

---

5. Train and evaluate the K-Nearest Neighbors Classifier model:

PYTHON CODE

```
# Firstly, we create an instance of the KNeighborsClassifier class.
This represents the K-Nearest Neighbors (KNN) algorithm, a type
of instance-based learning method used for classification. The
model classifies an object based on the majority class of its
'k' nearest neighbors. Here, we're using the default number of
neighbors, which is 5.
model_knn = KNeighborsClassifier()

# The 'fit' function is then used to train our KNN model using
the 'X_train' data and the corresponding survival statuses from
'train_data["Survived"]'.
model_knn.fit(X_train, train_data["Survived"])

# The 'score' function is applied to determine how accurately
our model predicts the survival statuses in our test dataset. It
```

compares the predicted results to the actual results in 'test_data["Survived"]', and returns the mean accuracy which we multiply by 100 to get a percentage. We round this percentage to 2 decimal places for a concise output and store this result in the 'KNN_score' variable.

```
KNN_score = round(model_knn.score(X_test, test_data["Survived"]) * 100, 2)
```

```
# The last line prints the string "K-Nearest Neighbors:" followed
by the accuracy of our K-Nearest Neighbors model contained in
the 'KNN_score' variable. This provides a human-friendly way of
understanding the model's accuracy.
print("K-Nearest Neighbors:", KNN_score)
```

PYTHON OUTPUT

K-Nearest Neighbors: 71.75

---

6. Train and evaluate the Support Vector Classifier model:

PYTHON CODE

```
# The initial line of the code generates an instance of the
Support Vector Classifier (SVC) class.
# The SVC is a type of Support Vector Machine (SVM) model, a
machine learning method often used for classification tasks. It
works by finding the hyperplane in a multi-dimensional space that
distinctly classifies the data points. Here, we're creating a SVC
model with the default parameters.
model_svc = SVC()
```

```python
# The 'fit' method is used to train the Support Vector Classifier
model using 'X_train' dataset and the corresponding survival
outcomes from 'train_data["Survived"]'.
model_svc.fit(X_train, train_data["Survived"])
# The 'score' function is utilized to evaluate how well the model
performs on the 'X_test' dataset.
# It calculates the mean accuracy of the model by comparing the
predicted survival outcomes to the actual outcomes in 'test_
data["Survived"]'. We multiply the accuracy by 100 to transform it
into a percentage and round it to two decimal points for a concise
result, storing it in the 'SVC_score' variable.
SVC_score = round(model_svc.score(X_test, test_
data["Survived"]) * 100, 2)

# The final line of the code prints the string "Support Vector
Classifier:" followed by the accuracy score of the SVC model. This
way, we can easily interpret the performance of the model.
print("Support Vector Classifier:", SVC_score)
```

PYTHON OUTPUT

Support Vector Classifier: 77.4

---

7. Train and evaluate the Logistic Regression model:

PYTHON CODE

```python
# We commence by initializing an instance of the
LogisticRegression class. Logistic Regression is a statistical
model that utilizes a logistic function to model a binary
```

dependent variable. In this case,# we're initializing a logistic regression model with its default parameters.

```
model_lr = LogisticRegression()
```

We call the 'fit' function to train the logistic regression model. We pass the training features 'X_train'# and the corresponding labels 'train_data["Survived"]' as inputs to this function. The model learns to classify whether a passenger survived or not based on the provided features and labels.

```
model_lr.fit(X_train, train_data["Survived"])
```

Next, the 'score' function is invoked on the trained model to evaluate its performance on the test data. The 'score' function returns the mean accuracy of the model predictions on the test data 'X_test' compared to the actual labels 'test_data["Survived"]'. We multiply the returned accuracy by 100 to convert it into a percentage and round it to 2 decimal places using 'round'. This accuracy score is then stored in 'LR_score'.

```
LR_score = round(model_lr.score(X_test, test_data["Survived"]) * 100, 2)
```

Finally, the accuracy score of our logistic regression model is printed out with a label "Logistic Regression:" for clear identification of the output. This gives us an understanding of the effectiveness of the model.

```
print("Logistic Regression:", LR_score)
```

PYTHON OUTPUT

Logistic Regression: 76.84

8. Train and evaluate the Decision Tree Classifier model:

PYTHON CODE

```
# To start, we instantiate a DecisionTreeClassifier. This signifies
that we're using a Decision Tree model which is a type of
flowchart-like structure where each internal node denotes a test
on an attribute, each branch signifies the outcome of the test, and
each leaf node (terminal node) holds a class label (a decision).
For the classifier, the decision is the predicted output.
model_dt = DecisionTreeClassifier()

# Next, we train our Decision Tree model. This is done by
utilizing the 'fit' function, which takes the training dataset 'X_
train' and the corresponding labels from 'train_data["Survived"]'.
The model then learns to classify the survival status based on the
attributes of the input data.
model_dt.fit(X_train, train_data["Survived"])

# We then use the 'score' function to estimate the performance of
our model on the test dataset. It compares the predicted results
for 'X_test' against the actual results in 'test_data["Survived"]',
and returns the mean accuracy. We convert this accuracy into a
percentage and round it off to 2 decimal places for a cleaner
output. This percentage is stored in 'DT_score'.
DT_score = round(model_dt.score(X_test, test_
data["Survived"]) * 100, 2)

# Lastly, we print the string "Decision Tree:" along with the
accuracy score of our Decision Tree model stored in 'DT_score'.
This way, we can easily grasp the effectiveness of our model.
print("Decision Tree:", DT_score)
```

PYTHON OUTPUT

Decision Tree: 68.36

IV. Next Steps and Discussion

1. Summarize the key takeaways from the lesson,
    including the importance of data preprocessing,
    train-test split, and model evaluation.

2. Discuss potential ways to improve model accuracy,
    such as feature engineering, hyperparameter
    tuning, and ensemble methods.

LESSON 20.
DATA ENGINEERING

Lesson Objectives:

The primary aim of this lesson is to introduce the critical role of data engineering in the domain of data science and machine learning. We aim to provide a solid foundation in techniques for data preprocessing, including handling missing data, feature engineering, and categorical data encoding. Students will learn how to extract, transform, and map data to improve data quality and ultimately the performance of a machine learning model. Additionally, we will cover the importance of feature selection, checking correlations, and understanding feature importance for refining model predictions.

Lesson Plan:

I. Introduction to Data Engineering

A. Explanation of the importance of data engineering in improving data quality and model performance

B. Overview of the techniques to be covered in the lesson

II. Data Engineering Techniques

A. Mapping Embarked port names to numerical values

B. Handling missing values in the Fare column

C. Extracting the Deck information from the Cabin column

D. Converting titles in the Name column to numerical values

E. Mapping gender values to numerical values

F. Creating a new column for the total number of relatives on board

G. Handling missing values in the Age column by generating random values

H. Binning the Age values into categories

I. Binning the Fare values into categories

III. Checking Correlations and Feature Importance

    A. Selecting the relevant features for analysis

    B. Calculating accuracy of the Random Forest Classifier model

    C. Calculating feature importances

    D. Displaying the top features based on importance

IV. Summary and Discussion

    A. Recap of the data engineering techniques covered

    B. Discuss the impact of data engineering on model performance and predictions

Lesson Description:

The lesson commences with an overview of the role of data engineering in enhancing data quality and model performance. This provides students with an understanding of the significance of data engineering in the data science lifecycle and the benefits it offers in terms of improving the performance of machine learning models.

Next, the lesson plunges into a practical demonstration of various data engineering techniques. We begin by mapping the 'Embarked' port names to numerical values, a process known as Label Encoding. This converts categorical data into a format that's more suitable for machine learning models. Next, we handle missing values in the 'Fare' column. Missing data treatment is an important aspect of data preprocessing and can greatly impact the performance of models.

Following this, we extract the 'Deck' information from the 'Cabin' column, showcasing an example of feature extraction. The ability to create new informative features from existing ones is a vital skill in data science. We then transform the titles in the 'Name' column to numerical values and map gender values likewise. The session further includes creating a new column for the total number of relatives onboard by adding 'SibSp' and 'Parch' columns, another instance of feature engineering.

The handling of missing values in the 'Age' column is addressed, followed by the binning of 'Age' and 'Fare' values into categories, offering a perspective on data discretization. This approach can help handle continuous variables and improve model performance.

The lesson moves forward to the concept of checking correlations and feature importance. We select the relevant features for analysis and calculate the accuracy of the Random Forest Classifier model. Then, feature importances are calculated using the `feature_importances_` attribute of the model. We display the top features based on importance, helping to identify which features are most influential in predicting the target variable.

The lesson wraps up with a summary of the data engineering techniques covered and a discussion on the impact of these techniques on model performance and predictions. This helps reinforce the techniques learned and their applications in improving model accuracy and reliability.

Detailed Lesson Notes:

I. Introduction to Data Engineering

1. Explain the importance of data engineering in improving data quality and model performance.
2. Provide an overview of the techniques to be covered in the lesson.

II. Data Engineering Techniques

1. Mapping Embarked port names to numerical values:

PYTHON CODE

```
# We start by creating a Python dictionary 'ports'. This
dictionary maps 'S', 'C', and 'Q', the different ports of
embarkation in the Titanic dataset, to numerical values 0, 1, and
2 respectively. The reason behind this conversion is that machine
learning algorithms can work more efficiently with numerical data.
ports = {"S": 0, "C": 1, "Q": 2}


# Next, we run a loop over both 'train_data' and 'test_data'
datasets. This is performed by including both datasets in a Python
list and iterating over that list. This ensures that the following
mapping operation is applied consistently on both training and
testing data.
for data in [train_data, test_data]:
    # The 'map' function is then used to replace each instance
    of the port of embarkation in the 'Embarked' column with the
    corresponding numerical value defined in the 'ports' dictionary.
    This operation transforms the 'Embarked' column into a
    numerical format that is more suitable for machine learning
    algorithms. The transformed column replaces the old 'Embarked'
    column in the dataset.
    data['Embarked'] = data['Embarked'].map(ports)
```

---

2. Handling missing values in the Fare column:

PYTHON CODE

```
# The for loop iterates over two datasets: 'train_data' and 'test_
data'. We include both datasets in a list, allowing us to process
the 'Fare' column in each dataset in a consistent manner. This
ensures uniformity in the way we handle missing values and data
types in both training and testing data.
for data in [train_data, test_data]:

    # Inside the loop, we first use the 'fillna' method on the 'Fare'
    column to fill any missing or NaN values with zero. The 'Fare'
    column represents the fare passengers paid for their journey
    on the Titanic. Occasionally, some fare information might be
    missing from the datasets. To handle this, we substitute these
    missing values with zero.
    data['Fare'] = data['Fare'].fillna(0)

    # Subsequently, we use the 'astype' method to convert or cast
    the 'Fare' column to integer data type. Even though fare is
    a numerical value, it could have been recorded as a floating-
    point number due to varying costs. However, for our analysis,
    we might decide that a simple integer value is sufficient
    and could simplify our model. Therefore, we make this
    transformation.
    data['Fare'] = data['Fare'].astype(int)
```

---

3. Extracting the Deck information from the Cabin column:

PYTHON CODE

```
# The 're' library is imported to use regular expressions, which
are sequences of characters that form a search pattern. This will
be used later to extract deck information from the 'Cabin' column.
import re

# The 'deck' dictionary maps the deck letters (from A to G and
an unknown category 'U') found on the Titanic to corresponding
numerical values, enabling us to represent the deck information in
a numeric format.
deck = {"A": 0, "B": 1, "C": 2, "D": 3, "E": 4, "F": 5,
"G": 6, "U": 7}

# We iterate over the 'train_data' (training data) and 'test_data'
(testing data) dataframes to uniformly process the 'Cabin' and
'Deck' columns.
for data in [train_data, test_data]:

    # The 'fillna' method replaces missing or NaN values in the
    'Cabin' column with "UN", signifying 'Unknown'.
    data['Cabin'] = data['Cabin'].fillna("UN")

    # Here, we generate a new column 'Deck'. We apply the 'map'
    function to the 'Cabin' column with a lambda function that
    extracts the alphabetical characters in each cabin number
    using regular expressions.

    # These alphabets represent the deck levels on the Titanic.
```

```python
data['Deck'] = data['Cabin'].map(lambda x: re.compile("([a-zA-Z]+)").search(x).group())
```

```python
# Then, we transform the 'Deck' column from alphabetic
# deck levels to numeric values using the 'deck' dictionary
# defined earlier.
data['Deck'] = data['Deck'].map(deck)
```

```python
# In case there are still any missing values after this
# transformation, we fill them with the numeric value 8,
# indicating an unknown deck level.
data['Deck'] = data['Deck'].fillna(8)
```

```python
# Lastly, we ensure that all the data in the 'Deck' column
# are of integer data type for consistency and efficiency in
# subsequent processing.
data['Deck'] = data['Deck'].astype(int)
```

4. Converting titles in the Name column to numerical values:

PYTHON CODE

```python
# This code  extracts the title from each passenger's name, which
# can provide valuable insights into their status and, potentially,
# their likelihood of survival.
```

```python
# We begin by defining a dictionary, 'titles', that maps
# common titles found in the 'Name' column to numerical values.
# This is done for easier handling of the data by machine
# learning algorithms.
```

```python
titles = {"Mr": 0, "Ms": 1, "Mrs": 2,"Other": 3}

# The code then iterates over the 'train_data' and 'test_data'
# DataFrames to process the 'Name' and 'Title' columns uniformly.
for data in [train_data, test_data]:

    # The 'extract' method along with a regular expression is used
    # to extract the title from the 'Name' column.
    # This is based on the fact that a title always ends
    # with a period.
    data['Title'] = data.Name.str.extract(' ([A-Za-z]+)\.',
    expand=False)

    # The 'replace' method is used to group rare titles and some
    # other common titles under a unified category 'Other'.
    data['Title'] = data['Title'].replace(['Lady', 'Countess','Capt',
    'Col','Don', 'Dr', 'Major', 'Rev', 'Sir', 'Jonkheer', 'Dona',
    'Master'], 'Other')

    # 'Mlle' and 'Miss' are French titles that are equivalent to
    # 'Ms', so these are replaced for consistency.
    data['Title'] = data['Title'].replace('Mlle', 'Ms')
    data['Title'] = data['Title'].replace('Miss', 'Ms')

    # 'Mme' is a French title equivalent to 'Mrs', so it is also
    # replaced for consistency.
    data['Title'] = data['Title'].replace('Mme', 'Mrs')

    # The 'map' function is then used to convert the title names
    # into numerical form using the 'titles' dictionary.
    data['Title']= data['Title'].map(titles)
```

```
# Finally, if there are any missing values after this
transformation, we fill them with the numeric value 4,
indicating an unknown title.
data['Title'] = data['Title'].fillna(4)
```

---

5. Mapping gender values to numerical values:

PYTHON CODE

```
# This code is focused on transforming the 'Sex' feature from a
categorical to a numerical form.
# Such transformation is important because machine learning
algorithms typically require numerical input and output variables.

# We start by creating a Python dictionary 'genders' which maps
'male' to 0 and 'female' to 1.
genders = {"male": 0, "female": 1}
# We then iterate over both the 'train_data' and 'test_data'
DataFrames to apply the transformation uniformly across the
entire dataset.
for data in [train_data, test_data]:

    # We use the 'map' function to replace the 'male' and 'female'
    strings in the 'Sex' column with their corresponding numerical
    values as defined in the 'genders' dictionary.
    data['Sex'] = data['Sex'].map(genders)
```

---

6. Creating a new column for the total number of
   relatives on board:

PYTHON CODE

```
# This piece of code centers around creating a new feature
'Relatives' that signifies the total number of family members
a passenger has on board. This can be insightful since
individuals with family might have behaved differently during the
crisis situation.
# We iterate over both 'train_data' and 'test_data' DataFrames to
ensure the new feature is created in both datasets.
for data in [train_data, test_data]:

    # 'SibSp' column in the dataset indicates the number of
    siblings or spouses a passenger has aboard. Similarly, 'Parch'
    denotes the number of parents or children a passenger is
    traveling with. We add these two columns to get the total
    count of family members a passenger has on the ship, creating
    a new column 'Relatives'.
    data['Relatives'] = data['SibSp'] + data['Parch']
```

7. Handling missing values in the Age column by
   generating random values:

PYTHON CODE

```
# This code is designed to handle missing values in the 'Age'
column of the data. It's filling the missing age values with random
numbers generated within one standard deviation from the mean,
giving us a statistically reasonable replacement.

# Iterating through both 'train_data' and 'test_data' DataFrames.
```

```
for data in [train_data, test_data]:

    # Calculate the mean and standard deviation of the 'Age'
    column in the current DataFrame.
    mean = data["Age"].mean()
    std = data["Age"].std()

    # Count the number of null (missing) values in the
    'Age' column.
    isNull = data["Age"].isnull().sum()

    # Generate an array of random integers within one standard
    deviation from the mean.
    # The size of this array is equal to the number of missing
    values in the 'Age' column.
    rand_age = np.random.randint(mean - std, mean + std,
    size=isNull)

    # Copy the 'Age' column into a new Series.
    age = data["Age"].copy()

    # Replace the NaN values in 'age' with the random
    ages generated.
    age[np.isnan(age)] = rand_age

    # Replace the original 'Age' column with our new 'age' that has
    no missing values.
    data["Age"] = age

    # Convert the 'Age' column to integer data type, as age is
    typically represented as whole numbers and this may aid in
    further analysis or modeling.
```

```
data["Age"] = data["Age"].astype(int)
```

---

8. Binning the Age values into categories:

PYTHON CODE

```
# This code is designed to categorize the 'Age' into different
groups. These groups or 'bins' are created based on the age range
they fall in. This kind of categorization or binning can be
helpful in machine learning models as it can sometimes improve
the model's performance by turning a continuous feature into a
categorical one.

# Iterating through both 'train_data' and 'test_data' DataFrames.
for data in [train_data, test_data]:

    # Converting the 'Age' column to integer data type. This is
    done as age is typically represented in whole numbers.
    data["Age"] = data["Age"].astype(int)

    # Replacing actual age with age groups/bins based on the age
    range they fall in.
    # Here, we define six groups:
    # Age 0: <= 15
    # Age 1: > 15 and <= 25
    # Age 2: > 25 and <= 35
    # Age 3: > 35 and <= 45
    # Age 4: > 45 and <= 65
    # Age 5: > 65
```

```
data.loc[data["Age"] <= 15, 'Age'] = 0
data.loc[(data['Age'] > 15) & (data['Age'] <= 25), 'Age'] = 1
data.loc[(data['Age'] > 25) & (data['Age'] <= 35), 'Age'] = 2
data.loc[(data['Age'] > 35) & (data['Age'] <= 45), 'Age'] = 3
data.loc[(data['Age'] > 45) & (data['Age'] <= 65), 'Age'] = 4
data.loc[data["Age"] > 65, 'Age'] = 5
```

9. Binning the Fare values into categories:

PYTHON CODE

```
# The main idea behind this code is to convert continuous fare
values into specific fare groups. This is known as 'binning' or
'bucketing' and is useful in creating categories from continuous
features, which can sometimes enhance the performance of certain
machine learning models.

# The code is looping through both the 'train_data' and 'test_
data' datasets.
for data in [train_data, test_data]:

    # Based on the fare range they fall into, the actual fare
    values are replaced with fare group identifiers:
    # Fare Group 0: Fare <= 10
    # Fare Group 1: Fare > 10 and <= 18
    # Fare Group 2: Fare > 18 and <= 31
    # Fare Group 3: Fare > 31 and <= 50
    # Fare Group 4: Fare > 50
```

```
data.loc[data['Fare'] <= 10, 'Fare'] = 0
data.loc[(data['Fare'] > 10) & (data['Fare'] <= 18), 'Fare'] = 1
data.loc[(data['Fare'] > 18) & (data['Fare'] <= 31), 'Fare'] = 2
data.loc[(data['Fare'] > 31) & (data['Fare'] <= 50), 'Fare'] = 3
data.loc[data['Fare'] > 50, 'Fare'] = 4

# The fare is then converted to an integer data type, as group
identifiers are generally whole numbers.
data['Fare'] = data['Fare'].astype(int)
```

III. Checking Accuracy, Correlations and Feature Importance

1. Selecting the relevant features for analysis:

PYTHON CODE

```
# Defining the features to be used in the model

# The variable `features` is being assigned a list of column names
# These columns represent the features that will be used
in the model
features = ["Pclass", "Sex", "Relatives", "SibSp", "Parch", "Fare",
"Age", "Title", "Deck"]
```

2. Calculating accuracy of the Random Forest Classifier model:

```python
# Selecting the features from the training dataset and creating a
# copy to avoid any modifications to the original data
X = train_data[features].copy()

# Similarly, creating a copy of the 'Survived' column from the
# training data to form our target variable
y = train_data["Survived"].copy()

# Selecting the same set of features from the test dataset for
# consistency in prediction and creating a copy
X_test = test_data[features].copy()

# Creating a copy of the 'Survived' column from the test data,
# this will be used to evaluate the model's performance
y_test = test_data["Survived"].copy()

# Initializing the Random Forest Classifier model with a specific
# configuration n_estimators=100 specifies that the forest will
# contain 100 trees max_depth=5 sets the maximum depth of each tree
# in the forest to 5 random_state=1 ensures that the splits you
# generate are reproducible. Scikit-learn uses random permutations
# to generate the splits.
model_RF = RandomForestClassifier(n_estimators=100, max_depth=5,
random_state=1)

# Training the Random Forest model on the training data
model_RF.fit(X, y)

# Scoring the model on the test data
# The score method returns the accuracy of the model on
# the test data
```

```
# It's calculated as the fraction of the test set samples that are
correctly classified
# The result is then multiplied by 100 to get a percentage and
rounded to two decimal places
RF_score=round(model_RF.score(X_test,y_test)*100,2)
# Printing the model's accuracy score
print("Random forest accuracy score: " + str(RF_score))
```

3. Calculating feature importances:

PYTHON CODE

```
# We are creating a DataFrame 'importances' that stores the
importance of each feature in our model. This is done by mapping
feature names to their importance scores from the model.
importances = pd.DataFrame({'feature': X.columns, 'importance':
np.round(model_RF.feature_importances_, 3)})

# Sorting the 'importances' DataFrame in descending order of
importance and resetting the index to 'feature'.
importances = importances.sort_values('importance',
ascending=False).set_index('feature')
```

4. Displaying the top features based on importance:

PYTHON CODE

```
# 'importances' is a Pandas DataFrame that contains feature
importances as computed by an algorithm, such as a tree-based
machine learning model RandomForest.
# The 'head' function is used to get the first N rows from this
DataFrame or Series.
# Here, 'head(9)' will return the first 9 rows, which corresponds to
the top 9 features ranked by importance.
# This is often used for understanding which features are most
influential for a machine learning model.
importances.head(9)
```

PYTHON OUTPUT

	importance
feature	
Title	0.299
Sex	0.263
Pclass	0.099
Relatives	0.083
Fare	0.081
Deck	0.069
Age	0.049
SibSp	0.039
Parch	0.019

The feature importances derived from the machine learning model tell a compelling story about the Titanic dataset. The 'Title', having the highest score of 0.299, emphasizes the importance of socio-economic status and social hierarchy of that era – where a person's title could be a significant predictor of survival. 'Sex', with an importance of 0.263, reaffirms the "women and children first" protocol followed during the evacuation. 'Pclass', a proxy for socio-economic status, having a score of 0.099, indicates that passengers in higher classes likely had better chances of survival. Other influential features like 'Relatives' a combination of siblings, spouses, parents, children on board) and 'Fare' (related to the passenger class and perhaps cabin location) play substantial roles, reflecting that family connections and wealth could have been survival factors. Lesser influential factors such as 'Deck', 'Age', 'SibSp' (number of siblings/spouses aboard), and 'Parch' (number of parents/children aboard), though have lower scores, still provide nuanced details, like the deck's possible proximity to lifeboats impacting survival, or survival odds linked with age and family size on board.

IV. Summary and Discussion

1. Recap the data engineering techniques covered in the lesson and their impact on data quality and model performance.
2. Discuss the importance of feature engineering and its role in improving the accuracy of machine learning models.

LESSON 21.
BANK FRAUD DETECTION USING MACHINE LEARNING

Lesson Objectives:

The primary goal of this lesson is to enlighten students about the role and importance of fraud detection in various domains, and to underscore the significance of data preprocessing in achieving accurate fraud predictions. An emphasis will be placed on understanding the concept of imbalanced datasets, and the implications they can have on model accuracy, revealing that perfect accuracy scores are not always indicative of an ideal model. The lesson aims to provide students with the necessary tools and knowledge to leverage Python libraries, including Pandas and scikit-learn, for data handling and model training in the context of fraud detection.

Lesson Plan:

I. Introduction to Fraud Detection

    A. Explanation of fraud detection and its importance in various industries

    B. Overview of the dataset used for fraud prediction

II. Data Preprocessing

    A. Loading and splitting the dataset into training and testing sets

    B. Preparing the data for model training

    C. Removing irrelevant features and analyzing dataset length

III. Model Training and Evaluation

    A. Training different classifiers on the data

    B. Evaluating the model performance using accuracy scores

    C. Discussing the high accuracy and the need for further analysis

IV. Analyzing Imbalanced Dataset

A. Introducing the concept of an imbalanced dataset

B. Explaining the confusion matrix and its role in assessing model performance

C. Discussing the impact of an imbalanced dataset on model accuracy

V. Conclusion and Discussion

A. Summarizing the key points covered in the lesson

B. Discussing the challenges and considerations in fraud detection

C. Discuss the importance of analyzing imbalanced datasets and the impact on model accuracy.

Lesson Description:

The lesson commences with an introduction to fraud detection, explaining its pertinence in sectors such as finance, healthcare, and e-commerce. An overview of the dataset to be used for fraud prediction will also be given, demonstrating the real-world application of the concepts being taught.

We then transition into data preprocessing. The focus here is on the Python libraries Pandas and scikit-learn. Students will learn how to load datasets using the Pandas' `read_csv()` function and split them into training and testing sets with the scikit-learn's `train_test_split()` function. The critical importance of these steps in model training will be highlighted.

The lesson then takes students through the process of preparing data for model training, discussing the removal of irrelevant features using the Pandas' `drop()` function, and analyzing the length of the dataset with the Python's built-in `len()` function. The concept of feature selection and its impact on model performance will be explored.

Next, the lesson moves onto model training and evaluation. Different classifiers will be introduced, and students will learn how to train these classifiers on the preprocessed data using scikit-learn's `fit()` method. The evaluation of these models using accuracy scores with scikit-learn's `accuracy_score()` function will be discussed. Here, the lesson takes an interesting turn as we delve into why high accuracy doesn't always mean the model is perfect, leading us into the concept of imbalanced datasets.

Imbalanced datasets, a common issue in machine learning, will be thoroughly examined. Students will learn how an imbalance in the data can lead to misleading accuracy scores. The confusion matrix, a critical tool for model performance assessment, will be introduced. Students will understand how the confusion matrix can help identify inaccuracies in the model, specifically using scikit-learn's `confusion_matrix()` function. The lesson emphasizes that not all perfect results are indeed perfect, fostering a more nuanced understanding of model evaluation.

Finally, the lesson concludes with a recap of the key concepts covered, such as fraud detection, data preprocessing, model training, imbalanced datasets, and confusion matrix. Challenges and considerations in fraud detection will be discussed to give students a comprehensive understanding of the subject. They will be encouraged to further explore and research advanced fraud detection techniques, providing a path for continued learning.

Detailed Lesson Notes:

I.   Introduction to Fraud Detection

1. Explain the importance of fraud detection and its impact on various industries.

2. Introduce the dataset[1] used for fraud prediction and its relevance to real-world scenarios.
3. Download dataset and rename it to "F_data.csv"

II. Data Preprocessing

1. Load necessary libraries.

PYTHON CODE

```
# Import the 'numpy' library which provides functionality for
handling arrays and applying mathematical operations on them, it's
fundamental to scientific computation with Python.
import numpy as np


# Import 'pandas', a versatile data manipulation library in Python
that provides flexible data structures and data analysis tools.
import pandas as pd
# Import the 'RandomForestClassifier' from the 'sklearn.ensemble'
module. A Random Forest is an ensemble machine learning technique
that constructs multiple decision trees and merges them together
to obtain a more accurate and stable prediction.
from sklearn.ensemble import RandomForestClassifier


# Import the 'LogisticRegression' class from the 'sklearn.linear_
model' module. Logistic regression is a statistical model used in
binary classification where the output is a probability that the
given input point belongs to a certain class.
from sklearn.linear_model import LogisticRegression
```

---

1 https://www.kaggle.com/datasets/ealaxi/paysim1

```python
# Import the 'DecisionTreeClassifier' from the 'sklearn.tree'
# module. Decision trees are a type of# model used in data mining
# for deriving a strategy to reach a specific goal, its also a common
# model for machine learning.
from sklearn.tree import DecisionTreeClassifier

# Import the 'MinMaxScaler' from 'sklearn.preprocessing' module.
# This estimator scales and translates each feature individually
# such that it is in the given range on the training set, i.e
# between zero and one.
from sklearn.preprocessing import MinMaxScaler
```

2. Load and split the dataset into training and testing sets:

PYTHON CODE

```python
# Start by importing the data from the CSV file named "F_data.csv"
# into a pandas dataframe 'data'.
data = pd.read_csv("F_data.csv")
# Create a new dataframe 'train_data' from the original
# 'data' dataframe.
# We are taking a random 10% sample from the original data for
# the training set.
# The 'random_state' parameter set to 25 ensures that the random
# sampling is reproducible.
train_data = data.sample(frac=0.1, random_state=25)
# In this step, we create our initial test data set.
```

```python
# We drop the indices of 'train_data' from the original 'data'
dataframe, so that 'test_data' does not contain any data points
that are already in 'train_data'.
test_data = data.drop(train_data.index)

# From this initial test set, we sample another random 10% to
create our final test set.
# Again, the 'random_state' parameter ensures reproducibility of
the sampling process.
test_data = test_data.sample(frac=0.1, random_state=25)
```

---

3. Prepare the data for model training:

PYTHON CODE

```python
# Extract the 'isFraud' column from 'train_data' and store it in a
separate variable 'y'.
# This becomes the target variable for our training set.
y = train_data["isFraud"]

# Generate descriptive statistics of 'train_data' dataframe. This
includes central tendency, dispersion, and shape of distribution.
train_data.describe()

# Drop the 'isFraud' column from 'train_data' as we have
separated it earlier. 'axis=1' indicates that we are dropping a
column, not a row.
train_data=train_data.drop('isFraud', axis=1)
```

```python
# Similarly, extract the 'isFraud' column from 'test_data' and
# store it in a separate variable 'y_test'. This is the target
# variable for our test set.
y_test = test_data["isFraud"]
# Print the concise summary of 'train_data' dataframe. This
# includes the list of all columns with their respective data types
# and non-null values count.
print(train_data.info())

# Drop the 'isFraud' column from 'test_data' since we've already
# stored it separately.
test_data=test_data.drop('isFraud', axis=1)

# Delete the 'nameDest', 'nameOrig' and 'type' columns from 'train_
# data' dataframe as we might have deemed them unnecessary for
# further analysis.
del train_data['nameDest']
del train_data['nameOrig']
del train_data['type']

# Print the length (number of rows) of the 'train_data' dataframe
# for a quick check on data size.
print('train data length '+ str(len(train_data)))

# Similarly, delete the 'nameDest', 'nameOrig' and 'type' columns
# from 'test_data' dataframe.
del test_data['nameDest']
del test_data['nameOrig']
del test_data['type']

# Print the length (number of rows) of the 'test_data' dataframe
# for a quick check on data size.
print('test data length '+ str(len(test_data)))
```

```
# Create a copy of the 'train_data' dataframe and store it in 'X'.
This can be useful to keep the original data unchanged while we
modify 'X' for modeling.
X=train_data.copy()

# Similarly, create a copy of 'test_data' and store it in 'X_test'.
X_test=test_data.copy()
```

PYTHON OUTPUT

```
<class 'pandas.core.frame.DataFrame'>
Int64Index: 76405 entries, 519737 to 543986
Data columns (total 10 columns):
 #   Column          Non-Null Count  Dtype
---  ------          --------------  -----
 0   step            76405 non-null  int64
 1   type            76405 non-null  object
 2   amount          76405 non-null  float64
 3   nameOrig        76405 non-null  object
 4   oldbalanceOrg   76405 non-null  float64
 5   newbalanceOrig  76405 non-null  float64
 6   nameDest        76405 non-null  object
 7   oldbalanceDest  76405 non-null  float64
 8   newbalanceDest  76405 non-null  float64
 9   isFlaggedFraud  76405 non-null  float64
dtypes: float64(6), int64(1), object(3)
memory usage: 6.4+ MB
None
train data length 76405
test data length 68764
```

III. Model Training and Evaluation

1. Train different classifiers on the data and evaluate their performance:

PYTHON CODE

```python
# Initialize a Random Forest Classifier model. We specify the
number of trees in the forest (n_estimators) to be 100, maximum
depth of the tree (max_depth) to be 5, and set the seed for the
random number generator (random_state) to 1 for reproducibility.
model_rf = RandomForestClassifier(n_estimators=100, max_depth=5,
random_state=1)

# Fit the Random Forest model on the training dataset ('X' being
the features, 'y' the target).
model_rf.fit(X, y)

# Calculate the model accuracy score on the test data ('X_test' as
features, 'y_test' as target), multiply it by 100 for percentage,
and round it to 2 decimal places.
RF_score = round(model_rf.score(X_test, y_test) * 100, 2)

# Display the accuracy score of the Random Forest model.
print("Random Forest: " + str(RF_score))
# Initialize a Logistic Regression model. Here we're using the
default parameters.
model_lr = LogisticRegression()

# Fit the Logistic Regression model on the training dataset.
model_lr.fit(X, y)
```

```python
# Calculate and display the accuracy score of the Logistic
Regression model, similar to what we did for the Random
Forest model.
LR_score = round(model_lr.score(X_test, y_test) * 100, 2)
print("Logistic Regression: " + str(LR_score))


# Initialize a Decision Tree Classifier model with
default parameters.
model_dt = DecisionTreeClassifier()


# Fit the Decision Tree model on the training dataset.
model_dt.fit(X, y)


# Calculate and display the accuracy score of the Decision Tree
model in a similar fashion.
DT_score = round(model_dt.score(X_test, y_test) * 100, 2)
print("Decision Tree: " + str(DT_score))
```

PYTHON OUTPUT

Random Forest: 99.95
/usr/local/lib/python3.10/dist-packages/sklearn/linear_model/_
logistic.py:458:
ConvergenceWarning: lbfgs failed to converge (status=1):
STOP: TOTAL NO. of ITERATIONS REACHED LIMIT.

Increase the number of iterations (max_iter) or scale the data
as shown in:
    https://scikit-learn.org/stable/modules/preprocessing.html
Please also refer to the documentation for alternative
solver options:
    https://scikit-learn.org/stable/modules/linear_model.
html#logistic-regression

```
n_iter_i = _check_optimize_result(
```
Logistic Regression: 99.95

Decision Tree: 99.93

IV. Analyzing Imbalanced Dataset

1. Explain the confusion matrix and its role in assessing model performance:

PYTHON CODE

```python
# Import 'cross_val_predict' function from sklearn's model
# selection module. This is used to perform cross validation and
# provides predictions made on each test fold.
from sklearn.model_selection import cross_val_predict

# Import 'confusion_matrix' function from sklearn's metrics
# module. This function is used to compute the confusion matrix to
# evaluate the accuracy of a classification.
from sklearn.metrics import confusion_matrix

# Initialize a MinMaxScaler which scales and translates each
# feature individually such that it is in the given range on the
# training set, i.e. between zero and one.
scaler = MinMaxScaler()
# Compute the minimum and maximum to be used for later scaling by
# fitting the scaler with 'X', our training data.
scaler.fit(X)
```

```
# Scale the features 'X' using the computed minimum and maximum
from the previous step.
X = scaler.transform(X)


# Perform cross validation on our model 'model_rf' using 'X' as
our features and 'y' as our target. 'cv=3' performs a 3-fold cross
validation, meaning the training set is split into 3 sets, and for
each unique set, the model is trained using the remaining 2 sets
and tested on the unique set.
predictions = cross_val_predict(model_rf, X, y, cv=3)


# Compute the confusion matrix to evaluate the accuracy of the
Random Forest classification.
# The confusion matrix compares the actual target values 'y'
with the predicted target values from the cross validation
'predictions'.
confusion_matrix(y, predictions)
```

PYTHON OUTPUT

```
array([[76363,     0],
       [   41,     1]])
```

---

2. Introduce the concept of an imbalanced dataset
   and its impact on model accuracy:
   - An imbalanced dataset occurs when the classes
     to be predicted are not represented equally.

PYTHON CODE

```python
# Calculate the sum of the 'y' array, which represents the total
number of positive cases (assuming 'y' is a binary variable).
# Divide this sum by the total length of the 'y' array to
calculate the proportion of positive cases in the dataset.
# This can be particularly useful in understanding the imbalance
in our target variable, where imbalance refers to unequal
distribution of classes within a dataset.
y.sum()/len(y)
```

PYTHON OUTPUT

0.0005497022446174989

- In the realm of fraud detection, the prevalence of genuine transactions typically dwarfs the quantity of fraudulent ones by a considerable margin. This vast discrepancy creates a scenario where the fraudulent instances are akin to a drop in the ocean, creating a clear imbalance in the data representation.

3. Discuss the impact of an imbalanced dataset on model accuracy:
   - Imbalanced datasets can lead to biased models that prioritize the majority class.

- Models tend to have high accuracy on the majority class but may struggle to detect the minority class (fraudulent transactions in this case).

V. Conclusion and Discussion

1. Summarize the key points covered in the lesson, including the challenges and considerations in fraud detection.
2. Discuss the importance of analyzing imbalanced datasets and the impact on model accuracy.
3. Encourage further exploration and research in fraud detection techniques.
4. Answer any questions and facilitate a discussion on the topic.

Note:

While the 99.9% accuracy indicated by the code might appear impressive at first glance, it can potentially be misleading when dealing with an unbalanced dataset. This high accuracy might not be a reliable measure of the model's true performance, as it could be largely driven by the overrepresentation of a certain class in the data. Therefore, additional analysis and performance metrics are necessary to obtain a more holistic and accurate understanding of the model's predictive power.

LESSON 22.
TIC TAC TOE AND NOT LOSING STRATEGY

Lesson Objectives:

The primary goal of this lesson is to empower students with a firm understanding of algorithmic thinking through the engaging medium of Tic Tac Toe. Initially, students will gain a clear grasp of the game's rules, structure, and objectives. As the lesson progresses, they will put this theoretical knowledge into practice by engaging in actual games, encouraging the development of strategic thinking. From this gameplay, we will transition into discussing and creating a "not losing" strategy. By guiding students to examine the board's layout and possible moves, they'll be encouraged to formulate a strategy that minimizes the chances of an opponent's victory. The ultimate objective is to develop their abilities to analyze various game scenarios and devise a sequence of actions – essentially, an algorithm. Through active game analysis and reflection sessions, they'll learn to identify potential scenarios where a game can result in a draw and recognize the elements of optimal play. Furthermore, we aim to promote reflection on their strategies and experience, enabling them to become more effective problem solvers – an essential skill in computer science.

Lesson Plan:

I.   Introduction to Tic Tac Toe

    A. Briefly explain the game of Tic Tac Toe and its objective

    B. Discuss the basic rules and the layout of the game board

II. Playing Tic Tac Toe

    A. Divide the students into pairs or small groups

    B. Provide each group with a Tic Tac Toe board and game pieces (X and O)

C. Guide the students through a few rounds of playing the game

D. Emphasize the importance of strategic thinking and planning ahead

III. Developing a Not Losing Strategy

A. Introduce the enumeration of the Tic Tac Toe board: 1:2:3, 4:5:6, 7:8:9

B. Discuss the concept of a not losing strategy

C. Guide the students in analyzing the board positions and identifying potential winning moves for both players

D. Encourage the students to formulate a strategy to prevent the opponent from winning

IV. Game Analysis and Discussion

A. Analyze a few game scenarios and discuss the students' strategies

B. Identify cases where a player can force a draw (no winner)

C. Explain why, with optimal play from both players, a game of Tic Tac Toe can result in a draw

V. Practice and Reflection

A. Provide additional practice opportunities for the students to apply their not losing strategy

B. Encourage students to reflect on their strategies and discuss their experiences

C. Address any questions or concerns raised by the students

Lesson Description:

In this lesson, students will learn how to play Tic Tac Toe and develop a not losing strategy. They will understand the enumeration of the Tic Tac Toe board and explore various board positions to identify winning moves and prevent the opponent from winning. The lesson will also address the concept of a draw (no winner) and explain why it can occur even when both players are using the right strategy.

Detailed Lesson Notes:

1. Begin by briefly explaining the game of Tic Tac Toe and its objective. Emphasize that the goal is to get three of their own game pieces (X or O) in a row, either horizontally, vertically, or diagonally.

2. Discuss the basic rules and the layout of the Tic Tac Toe board, which consists of a 3x3 grid.

3. Divide the students into pairs or small groups and provide each group with a Tic Tac Toe board and game pieces (X and O).

4. Guide the students through a few rounds of playing the game, ensuring they understand the rules and take turns placing their game pieces on the board.

5. Emphasize the importance of strategic thinking and planning ahead. Encourage the students to analyze the board and anticipate their opponent's moves.

6. Introduce the enumeration of the Tic Tac Toe board: 1:2:3, 4:5:6, 7:8:9. Explain that this numbering system is helpful for formalizing strategies and analyzing different board positions.

7. Discuss the concept of a not losing strategy, which aims to prevent the opponent from winning rather than solely focusing on winning. Emphasize the importance of blocking the opponent's winning moves.

8. Guide the students in analyzing the board positions and identifying potential winning moves for both players. Encourage them to consider different scenarios and think ahead.

9. Facilitate a class discussion to help students formulate a not losing strategy. Encourage them to share their ideas and reasoning behind their strategies.

10. Analyze a few game scenarios and discuss the students' strategies. Identify cases where a player can force a draw (no winner) by making the right moves.

11. Explain that, with optimal play from both players, a game of Tic Tac Toe can result in a draw. Highlight the characteristics of such games and why it is challenging to achieve a win in those scenarios.

12. Provide additional practice opportunities for the students to apply their not losing strategy. Encourage them to play against different opponents and refine their strategies.

13. Conclude the lesson by allowing students to reflect on their strategies and experiences. Address any questions or concerns raised by the students and provide clarifications if needed.

LESSON 23.
TEACHING THE COMPUTER TO PLAY TIC TAC TOE

Lesson Objectives:

The purpose of this lesson is to introduce students to the principles of game development in Python, using the popular game Tic Tac Toe as a basis. They will also learn the essentials of artificial intelligence (AI) as it applies to gaming. Students will learn to design the game board, check for a winner or if the board is full, manage player and computer turns, and set up the game execution loop. By the end of the lesson, students will be able to design, implement, and analyze a basic AI game in Python.

Lesson Plan:

I.   Introduction to the Game and AI

A. Briefly explain the game of Tic Tac Toe and its objective.
B. Discuss the concept of AI and its role in playing games.

II. Drawing the Tic Tac Toe Board

A. Introduce the `draw_board(board)` function.
   - Use the provided code as an example.
B. Guide students in understanding the code and how it displays the board.
C. Encourage students to run the code and observe the board.

III. Checking for a Winner or Full Board

A. Introduce the `check_winner(board)` and `check_full_board()` functions.
   - Use the provided code for checking winner and full board.
B. Discuss how these functions determine the game outcome.
C. Guide students in understanding the code and its role in ending the game.

IV. Player's Turn

A. Explain the code for the player's turn.
  - Use the provided code for the player's turn (box selection and input validation).
B. Guide students in understanding the input validation and updating the board.
C. Encourage students to play the game against the computer.

V. Computer's Turn

A. Explain use of random number generator for the computer's turn.
B. Discuss possible algorithm for the AI to make moves.
C. Guide students in understanding the logic and decision-making process.
D. Encourage students to observe the computer's moves and analyze its strategy.

VI. Game Execution

A. Walk students through the code for the game execution.
  - Use the provided code for the game execution (loop, player's turn, computer's turn).
B. Encourage students to run the code and play against the computer.

> C. Discuss the outcomes and strategies used by both players.

VII. Reflection and Discussion

> A. Reflect on the game results and experiences.
> C. Encourage students to propose AI algorithm to fully automate game play.

Lesson Description:

Our exploration begins with an introduction to the concept of Tic Tac Toe, delineating its objectives. This will be supplemented by an exposition on Artificial Intelligence (AI) and the pivotal role it plays in gaming scenarios. We will underscore the relevance of AI in streamlining gameplay, delivering captivating experiences, and simulating strategic cognition. This lesson was inspired by an insightful article on Medium penned by Esteban Thillez[1]. While we acknowledge that the provided Python code may not be optimal from a software engineering perspective, we believe it corresponds to the coding experience of school children and effectively illustrates the underlying algorithms.

---

1 https://medium.com/@estebanthi/tic-tac-toe-game-in-python-for-beginners-6c09bb63eb84

Our first hands-on segment dives into the intricacies of sketching the Tic Tac Toe game board. Here, we demystify the Python function draw_board(board). It ingeniously employs lists and print statements to render the board visually. We will guide students to fathom the interaction between this function and the game board data, which together birth a visual representation. As part of this process, they will be urged to execute the function, inspect the output, and tinker with varied inputs.

In the subsequent section, we clarify the game's termination conditions by introducing the functions check_winner(board) and check_full_board(). These functions peruse the board's content to recognize a winner or to ascertain if all positions have been occupied. Students will gain insights into how these functions steer the game progression and cessation. This elucidates the Python concepts of loops, conditionals, and list manipulation.

Further, we dissect the player's turn, studying the code responsible for accepting and validating the player's input. We discuss a function that not only ensures appropriate box selection but also updates the board after each move. This segment exposes students to Python's input handling and exception management mechanisms. To foster an experiential learning environment, we advocate for students to engage in a round of gameplay.

We then pivot our attention to the computer's turn. In this segment, students will learn about Python's random number generator and its role in determining the computer's moves. A simple algorithm, wherein the computer selects a random empty slot for its move, is discussed. Here, students are introduced to the Python random library and its randint() function, alongside AI principles.

In the final execution phase, we amalgamate all the functions previously elaborated on. Students will witness the entire game flow, ranging from the board's inception and player moves to the winner identification and game cessation. The crucial role of the game loop, where Python's while loop serves as the backbone, is accentuated. To fully comprehend the different code segments in action, students are encouraged to engage in a full-fledged game against the computer.

To conclude, we will reflect upon the game outcomes, discussing the strategies employed by both players and the AI's role. Students will also be stimulated to contemplate ways to augment the AI algorithm for more strategic gameplay. This final discussion segment prompts critical thinking about AI and game strategies, thereby igniting ideas for potential future game development projects.

Detailed Lesson Notes:

I.   Introduction to the Game and AI

- Explain that Tic Tac Toe is a game played on a 3x3 grid, where the goal is to get three of your symbols (X or O) in a row, either horizontally, vertically, or diagonally.
- Discuss the concept of AI and its ability to make strategic decisions in games.
- Set up the environment

PYTHON CODE

```python
# The random module is imported, providing the ability to generate
a random number.
import random

# This list represents the game board. Each string stands for a
cell in a 3x3 Tic Tac Toe board.
board = [
    "", "", "",
    "", "", "",
    "", "", ""
]

# The winner variable will be used to store the winner of the
game. Initially, it is empty.
winner = ""
```

```
# The full_board variable will be used to keep track if the game
board is filled or not. It starts as False.
full_board = False
```

II. Drawing the Tic Tac Toe Board

- Introduce the `draw_board(board)` function to display the Tic Tac Toe board.
- Use the provided code as an example and explain how it prints the board and symbols.
- Run the code together and encourage students to observe the board.

PYTHON CODE

```
# This function is used to display the current state of the board
to the user.
def draw_board(board):

    # Iterate over the board to print the board with the
    current marks.
    for index, box in enumerate(board):

        # At the beginning of every new row, print a row separator.
        if index // 3 != (index - 1) // 3:
          print("+---+---+---+")

        # If the box is filled, print the value. Else, print an
        empty space.
        if box:
```

```
    print("| " + box + " ", end="")

  else:
   print("|    ", end="")

  # At the end of every row, print a column separator.
  if index % 3 == 2:
   print("|")

  # At the end of the last row, print a row separator.
  if index == 8:
   print("+---+---+---+")
```

III. Checking for a Winner or Full Board

- Introduce the `check_winner(board)` and `check_full_board()` functions, as provided in the lesson notes.
- Discuss how these functions determine the game outcome by checking for a winning configuration or a full board.
- Guide students in understanding the code and its role in ending the game.

PYTHON CODE

```
# This function checks the winning conditions of the game. It
checks for any filled row, column, or diagonal.
def check_winner(board):
```

```python
# Check for horizontal wins.
if board[0] == board[1] == board[2] != "":
    return board[0]
if board[3] == board[4] == board[5] != "":
    return board[3]
if board[6] == board[7] == board[8] != "":
    return board[6]

# Check for vertical wins.
if board[0] == board[3] == board[6] != "":
    return board[0]
if board[1] == board[4] == board[7] != "":
    return board[1]
if board[2] == board[5] == board[8] != "":
    return board[2]

# Check for diagonal wins.
if board[0] == board[4] == board[8] != "":
    return board[0]
if board[2] == board[4] == board[6] != "":
    return board[2]

# This function checks if the board is filled or not by counting
# filled cells.
def check_full_board():
    counter = 0

    # Iterate through the board. For every filled cell, increment
    # the counter.
    for box in board:
        if box:
            counter += 1
```

```
# If all the cells are filled, return True. Else, return False.
if counter == 9:
    return True
return False
```

IV. Player's Turn

- Explain the code for the player's turn, as provided in the lesson notes.
- Discuss how the code prompts the player to select a box and validates the input.
- Guide students in understanding how the board is updated with the player's symbol (X).
- Encourage students to play the game against the computer and practice their moves.

PYTHON CODE

```
# Initialize values for player's move.
box_number = -1
valid_input = False
while not valid_input:

    # Prompt the player to make a move.
    box_number = int(input("Choose a box"))

    # Validate the player's input.
    if box_number < 1 or box_number > 9:
        print("Please choose a box between 1 and 9")

    # Validate if the chosen cell is empty.
```

```
    elif board[box_number - 1]:
        print("Please choose an empty box")

    else:
        # Make the player's move and set valid_input to True.
        board[box_number - 1] = "X"
        valid_input = True

# Check if there is a winner after the player's move.
winner = check_winner(board)

# Update the state of the full_board variable.
full_board = check_full_board()

# If there is a winner or the board is full, break the loop.
if winner or full_board:
    break
```

V. Computer's Turn

- Explain the code for the computer's turn, as provided in the lesson notes.
- Discuss the AI algorithm used to make the computer's moves.
- Guide students in understanding the logic and decision-making process of the algorithm.
- Encourage students to observe the computer's moves and analyze its strategy.

PYTHON CODE

```python
# Initialize values for computer's move.
computer_play = -1
while board[computer_play - 1] or computer_play == -1:

    # Computer makes a random move.
    computer_play = random.randint(1, 9)

# Mark the computer's move on the board.
board[computer_play - 1] = "O"

# Print the computer's move.
print("Computer played box " + str(computer_play))

# Check if there is a winner after the computer's move.
winner = check_winner(board)

# Update the state of the full_board variable.
full_board = check_full_board()

# If there is a winner or the board is full, break the loop.
if winner or full_board:
    break
```

VI. Game Execution

- Walk students through the code for the game execution, as provided in the lesson notes.

- Discuss the game loop, alternating between the player's turn and the computer's turn.
- Encourage students to run the code and play against the computer, analyzing the outcomes and strategies used.

PYTHON CODE

```python
# The game loop starts here. It runs until there is a winner or
the board is full.
while not winner and not full_board:

    # Draw the current state of the board.
    draw_board(board)

    # Initialize values for player's move.
    box_number = -1
    valid_input = False
    while not valid_input:

        # Prompt the player to make a move.
        box_number = int(input("Choose a box"))

        # Validate the player's input.
        if box_number < 1 or box_number > 9:
            print("Please choose a box between 1 and 9")

        # Validate if the chosen cell is empty.
        elif board[box_number - 1]:
            print("Please choose an empty box")
```

```python
    else:
        # Make the player's move and set valid_input to True.
        board[box_number - 1] = "X"
        valid_input = True

# Check if there is a winner after the player's move.
winner = check_winner(board)

# Update the state of the full_board variable.
full_board = check_full_board()

# If there is a winner or the board is full, break the loop.
if winner or full_board:
    break

# Initialize values for computer's move.
computer_play = -1
while board[computer_play - 1] or computer_play == -1:

    # Computer makes a random move.
    computer_play = random.randint(1, 9)

# Mark the computer's move on the board.
board[computer_play - 1] = "O"

# Print the computer's move.
print("Computer played box " + str(computer_play))

# Check if there is a winner after the computer's move.
winner = check_winner(board)

# Update the state of the full_board variable.
```

```python
    full_board = check_full_board()

    # If there is a winner or the board is full, break the loop.
    if winner or full_board:
        break
# At the end of the game, print the game board one final time and
declare the result.
if winner:
    draw_board(board)
    print(winner + " is a winner!")
else:
    print("No winner")
```

PYTHON OUTPUT

```
+---+---+---+
|   |   |   |
+---+---+---+
|   |   |   |
+---+---+---+
|   |   |   |
+---+---+---+
Choose a box
```

VII. Reflection and Discussion

- Reflect on the game results and experiences.
- Encourage students to propose AI algorithm to fully automate gameplay

LESSON 24.
STEPPING UP THE GAME: IMPLEMENTING STRATEGIC AI

Lesson Objectives:

The goal of this lesson is to introduce students to the development and implementation of an artificial intelligence (AI) algorithm that manages the computer's moves in the game of Tic Tac Toe. Students will learn the underlying logic used to decide the computer's moves, and how to incorporate this AI into the existing game code. By the end of this lesson, students will have a deeper understanding of AI game strategy, be capable of using control flow tools to build decision-making logic, and enhance their ability to develop AI for simple games.

Lesson Plan:

I. Review of Previous Lesson

A. Briefly revisit the concepts from the previous lesson.
B. Discuss the importance of AI in automating gameplay.

II. Introduction to AI Decision-Making

A. Explain the purpose of the new AI algorithm in deciding the computer's moves.
B. Discuss the concept of decision trees in AI.

III. Understanding the AI Code

A. Explain the functions `make_move()` and `is_space_free()`.
   - Discuss their role in the algorithm.
B. Introduce the `choose_move()` function.
   - Discuss how it selects a valid move.
C. Explore the `get_computer_move()` function.
   - Break down the decision-making process for the AI.

IV. Implementing the AI Algorithm

A. Guide students in integrating the new AI functions into the existing game code.
B. Explain the changes in the game execution loop.

V. Testing the AI

    A. Encourage students to run the new game code.

    B. Analyze the behavior of the AI during gameplay.

VI. Reflection and Discussion

    A. Reflect on the AI's decision-making process and its effectiveness.

    B. Discuss possibilities for further improvements and enhancements to the AI.

Lesson Description:

In this lesson, we begin by revisiting the Tic Tac Toe game from the previous lesson, with emphasis on the role of AI in automating gameplay. We then shift focus to decision-making in AI, setting the context for the upcoming code walkthrough.

Next, we start analyzing the AI algorithm's code. We begin with the `make_move()` and `is_space_free()` functions. These functions allow the AI to place its letter on the board and to verify if a given space is available. These are fundamental to the AI's operation.

We then delve into the `choose_move()` function. This function looks through a set of possible moves, and selects a valid one based on board availability. We examine how this function enables the AI to choose a move from potential options.

Following this, we dissect the heart of the AI: the `get_computer_move()` function. This function represents the decision tree of the AI's gameplay strategy. It prioritizes winning the game, then blocking the player from winning, then occupying the center square, then occupying a corner, and finally moving to a side. By breaking down each decision point, we explore how the AI prioritizes its moves and how it implements strategic gameplay.

Next, we guide the students in integrating the new AI algorithm into the existing Tic Tac Toe game. The key change here is replacing the previous random move selection with a call to `get_computer_move()` in the game execution loop. This modification gives the AI control over the computer's moves.

We then invite the students to run the updated game and observe the behavior of the AI. Students will experience firsthand the game's evolution, from random moves to a strategic adversary.

The lesson concludes with a reflection on the AI's decision-making process and its performance during the gameplay. A discussion on possible enhancements and improvements to the AI will give students an insight into the continuous development and learning process in AI game programming.

Detailed Lesson Notes:

I. Review of Previous Lesson

    A. In our last lesson, we developed a simple AI for the Tic Tac Toe game where the computer made random moves.

    B. The AI we created, although simple, represents a fundamental concept in computer science – automating decision-making to create intelligent gameplay.

II. Introduction to AI Decision-Making

    A. Today, we're going to enhance our AI. Instead of making random moves, our AI will now analyze the board and make strategic decisions.

B. These decisions will be based on a simplified form of a decision tree, where the AI assesses multiple scenarios and chooses the best course of action.

III. Understanding the AI Code

A. Let's begin by examining the helper functions `make_move()` and `is_space_free()`. These functions allow the AI to interact with the game board – placing a move on the board and checking if a space is available, respectively.

PYTHON CODE

```python
def make_move(board, letter, move):
    # Places the given letter at the given move position on the board.
    board[move] = letter


def is_space_free(board, move):
    # Checks if a given move position on the board is free.
    return board[move] == ''
```

B. The `choose_move()` function allows the AI to choose a valid move from a list of potential moves.

PYTHON CODE

```python
def choose_move(board, moves):
```

```
# Creates a list of possible moves by checking if each move in
the provided list is free.
possibleMoves = []
for i in moves:
  if is_space_free(board, i):
    possibleMoves.append(i)

# If there are any possible moves, choose a random one.
Otherwise, return None.
if len(possibleMoves) != 0:
  return random.choice(possibleMoves)
else:
  return None
```

C. The heart of our AI algorithm is the `get_computer_move()` function. It breaks down into several steps:

PYTHON CODE

```python
def get_computer_move(board, computerLetter, playerLetter):
  # Step 1: Check if the AI can win with the next move.
  for i in range(0, 9):
    copy = [i for i in board]
    if is_space_free(copy, i):
      make_move(copy, computerLetter, i)
      if check_winner(copy) == computerLetter:
        return i
```

```python
# Step 2: Check if the player could win with their next move
# and block them.
for i in range(0, 9):
    copy = [i for i in board]
    if is_space_free(copy, i):
        make_move(copy, playerLetter, i)
        winner = check_winner(copy)
        if str(winner) == playerLetter:
            return i

# Step 3: Try to take the center square if it's free.
if is_space_free(board, 4):
    return 4

# Step 4: Try to take one of the corners.
move = choose_move(board, [0, 2, 6, 8])
if move != None:
    return move

# Step 5: Take one of the sides.
return choose_move(board, [1, 3, 5, 7])
```

IV. Implementing the AI Algorithm

A. Now we will integrate these new functions into our existing game code. Instead of the computer choosing a random valid move, it will now use our `get_computer_move()` function to select a move.

B. Our game execution loop will now change slightly with the new AI code. The computer's turn will now be a call to our new function as shown below:

PYTHON CODE

```
# Display the current state of the game board
draw_board(board)

# Get the computer's move based on the current board state
# The `get_computer_move` function takes the board, computer's
symbol ("O"), and player's symbol ("X") as parameters
computer_play = get_computer_move(board, "O", "X")

# Update the board by placing the computer's symbol ("O") at the
chosen position
board[computer_play] = "O"

# Print a message indicating which box the computer played
print("The computer played box " + str(computer_play + 1))
```

PYTHON OUTPUT

```
+---+---+---+
|   |   |   |
+---+---+---+
|   | O |   |
+---+---+---+
|   |   |   |
+---+---+---+
The computer played box 9
```

C. Review the full code of the game.

PYTHON CODE

```python
import random

# Initialize an empty tic-tac-toe board. Each string in the list
represents a cell on the board.
board = [
    "", "", "",
    "", "", "",
    "", "", ""
]


# Variable to hold the letter (either "X" or "O") of the winning
player. Initially empty, as no player has won yet.
winner = ""


# Boolean variable to keep track of whether the board is full
or not. Initially set to False because the board is empty at the
start of the game.
full_board = False
# Define a function to check the current state of the game board
for a winner.
def check_winner(board):

    # This function checks all rows, columns, and diagonals to see
if any of them contain the same letter (and are not empty), which
would mean a player has won.

    if board[0] == board[1] == board[2] != "":
        return board[0]  # Top row
```

```python
    if board[3] == board[4] == board[5] != "":
        return board[3]   # Middle row
    if board[6] == board[7] == board[8] != "":
        return board[6]   # Bottom row
    if board[0] == board[3] == board[6] != "":
        return board[0]   # Left column
    if board[1] == board[4] == board[7] != "":
        return board[1]   # Middle column
    if board[2] == board[5] == board[8] != "":
        return board[2]   # Right column
    if board[0] == board[4] == board[8] != "":
        return board[0]   # Diagonal from top left
    if board[2] == board[4] == board[6] != "":
        return board[2]   # Diagonal from top right


# Define a function to check if the game board is full (i.e., all
cells have been filled with either "X" or "O").
def check_full_board():

    # This function counts the number of filled cells on the
board. If all 9 cells are filled, it returns True. Otherwise, it
returns False.
    counter = 0
    for box in board:
        if box:
            counter += 1
    if counter == 9:
        return True
    return False


# Define a function to draw the current state of the game board in
the console.
```

```python
def draw_board(board):

    # This function iterates through each cell in the board
    list. It adds border lines and cell contents to create a visual
    representation of the board.

    for index, box in enumerate(board):

        if index // 3 != (index - 1) // 3:  # Add a horizontal line
    at the start of each new row
            print("+---+---+---+")

        if box:  # If the current cell is not empty, add its
    contents ("X" or "O") to the cell
            print("| " + box + " ", end="")
        else:  # If the current cell is empty, add a blank
    space to the cell
            print("|   ", end="")

        if index % 3 == 2:  # Add a vertical line at the
    end of each row
            print("|")
        if index == 8:  # Add a horizontal line at the very bottom
    of the board
            print("+---+---+---+")

# Function to place a player's letter ("X" or "O") in a specific
cell on the board
def make_move(board, letter, move):
    board[move] = letter
# Function to check if a specific cell on the board is free (i.e.,
does not contain either "X" or "O")
```

```python
def is_space_free(board, move):
    return board[move] == ''


# Function to select a random move from a list of potential moves,
# provided the selected cell is free.
def choose_move(board, moves):
  possibleMoves = [i for i in moves if is_space_free(board, i)]
  return random.choice(possibleMoves) if possibleMoves else None


# Function to determine the computer's move using a basic
# AI algorithm
def get_computer_move(board, computerLetter, playerLetter):

  # First, the function checks if there's a move the computer can
  # make that would result in the computer winning the game.
  for i in range(0, 9):
    copy = [i for i in board]
    if is_space_free(copy, i):
      make_move(copy, computerLetter, i)
      if check_winner(copy)==computerLetter:
        return i
  # Next, the function checks if there's a move the player could
  # make on their next turn that would result in the player winning
  # the game. If such a move exists, the computer takes that move to
  # block the player from winning.
  for i in range(0, 9):
    copy = [i for i in board]
    if is_space_free(copy, i):
      make_move(copy, playerLetter, i)
      if check_winner(copy)==playerLetter:
        return i
```

```python
# If neither of the above scenarios apply, the function checks
if the center cell (cell 4) is free. If it is, the computer
takes that cell.
    if is_space_free(board, 4):
        return 4
    # If the center cell is not free, the function checks if any of
    the corner cells (cells 0, 2, 6, and 8) are free. If one is, the
    computer takes that cell.
    move = choose_move(board, [0, 2, 6, 8])
    if move != None:
        return move

    # If none of the corner cells are free, the function makes the
    computer take one of the remaining free cells (the "edge" cells:
    1, 3, 5, and 7).
    return choose_move(board, [1, 3, 5, 7])


# Game loop. This will keep the game running as long as there's no
winner and the board isn't full.
while not winner and not full_board:

    draw_board(board)  # Draw the current state of the board at
    the start of each iteration.


    # The following block of code handles the player's turn.
    The player is asked to choose a cell where they'd like to place
    their "X". The game will not proceed until the player enters a
    valid input (i.e., a number between 1 and 9 for a cell that isn't
    already occupied).
    box_number = -1
    valid_input = False
    while not valid_input:
```

```
    box_number = int(input("Choose a box"))
    if box_number < 1 or box_number > 9:
        print("Please choose a box between 1 and 9")
    elif board[box_number - 1]:
        print("Please choose an empty box")
    else:
        board[box_number - 1] = "X"
        valid_input = True
```

After the player has made their move, the game checks if there's a winner or if the board is full.

```
    winner = check_winner(board)
    full_board = check_full_board()
```

If the player's move resulted in a win for the player or a full board, the game loop ends.

```
    if str(winner)=='X' or full_board:
      break
```

If the game has not ended after the player's turn, it's the computer's turn. The computer decides on a move based on the AI algorithm defined earlier, and places an "O" in the chosen cell.

```
    draw_board(board)
    computer_play = get_computer_move(board, "O", "X")
    board[computer_play] = "O"
    print("Computer played box " + str(computer_play+1))
```

After the computer's move, the game checks once again if there's a winner or if the board is full.

```
    winner = check_winner(board)
    full_board = check_full_board()
```
Once the game loop ends, the game checks for a winner and prints a message indicating the result of the game.

```
win=str(winner)
if win != '' and win != 'None':
  print(win + " is a winner!")
else:
  print("No winner")
draw_board(board)
```

PYTHON OUTPUT

```
+---+---+---+
|   |   |   |
+---+---+---+
|   |   |   |
+---+---+---+
|   |   |   |
+---+---+---+
Choose a box
```

V.   Testing the AI

A. Let's run our enhanced game. You should see the computer making more strategic moves, making the game more challenging.

B. Pay close attention to the AI's moves. Try to understand the reasoning behind each move based on our algorithm.

VI. Reflection and Discussion

A. Reflect on the effectiveness of our new AI's decision-making process. Do you notice any specific patterns or behaviors?

B. Let's think about how we can further improve our AI. What additional strategies could we incorporate into our decision-making algorithm to make it even smarter?

CONCLUDING INSIGHTS AND LOOKING AHEAD

As we close this instructive journey through "Python and Machine Learning for Kids," let us take a moment to appreciate the knowledge, skills, and perspective that you, as parents and educators, have helped nurture in the young learners. This explorative odyssey from basic Python programming to the nuanced world of machine learning has armed our children with valuable tools for the digital age.

Guiding young minds through the labyrinth of Python programming, control structures, functions, and algorithms, you've unveiled the potential and practicality of programming. You've illuminated the role of machine learning in our everyday lives, encouraging them to probe data patterns, manipulate data using the powerful pandas library, and even predict outcomes based on existing data.

Together, we've shown them that coding extends beyond the act of writing lines of code. It encompasses logic, creativity, problem-solving, and resilience. With each encountered error and solved bug, they've developed a grit for debugging, fostering an attitude of determination that transcends far beyond the coding environment.

As we conclude this book, remember, this is merely the start of their adventure. With the firm foundation established here, the world of technology is a canvas for their curiosity and creativity. Whether their path leads them towards more advanced programming languages, complex machine learning algorithms, or burgeoning fields like artificial intelligence, their journey has been well seeded.

We are in an era where technology evolves at a breakneck speed, offering endless avenues for continuous learning. Encourage them to remain curious, to keep exploring, to challenge themselves, and to adapt to new paradigms. The ability to learn and adapt is invaluable in our rapidly transforming world.

The true essence of learning is not reaching a destination; instead, it lies in the journey itself. The challenges encountered, the mistakes made, the solutions found, the 'aha' moments experienced, and the growth witnessed – these are the true victories.

As educators and parents, our primary goal is to spark curiosity and instill a lifelong love of learning in our children. This book aimed to do just that – ignite an interest in coding and data science. It is our hope that the knowledge and skills they've gained will not only serve them in their future academic pursuits but will also empower them to leverage technology for problem-solving, innovation, and creating a brighter tomorrow.

As we bid adieu to this guide, let us look ahead with optimism and anticipation. May the seeds of curiosity sown today bloom into a lifelong quest for knowledge and innovation. The future belongs to those who believe in the power of their dreams. And our dream is to see every child equipped with the knowledge and skills to navigate the digital future confidently.

Keep teaching, keep inspiring, and remember – every great journey begins with a single step. Here's to many more exciting adventures in the realm of Python and machine learning!

Happy teaching, and until our paths cross again, continue to inspire the coders of tomorrow.

ABOUT THE AUTHOR

Dr. Igor Balk is a highly accomplished technology executive recognized for his expertise in driving innovative technological initiatives and fostering business growth. He holds a Ph.D. in Economics and possesses extensive academic knowledge in Electrical Engineering and Computer Science, acquired during his studies at the esteemed Massachusetts Institute of Technology (MIT).

With an exceptional ability to oversee intricate technological projects and lead machine learning and data analytics initiatives, Dr. Balk consistently leverages cutting-edge technologies such as AI, NLP, Computer Vision, and Predictive Analytics to achieve competitive advantages in the ever-evolving business landscape.

Dr. Balk's impressive accomplishments extend to his role as an inventor, holding multiple US patents that demonstrate his capacity for technological creativity and innovation. Moreover, he is a prolific author, producing an extensive body of scientific papers that delve into the practical applications of machine learning and data analytics.

In addition to his scholarly contributions, Dr. Balk actively shares his thought leadership at industry conferences, where he serves as a co-chair on topics ranging from data science and artificial intelligence to sustainability. Through this influential role, he actively shapes the dialogues that steer the future direction of technology in the business sphere.

www.ingramcontent.com/pod-product-compliance
Lightning Source LLC
LaVergne TN
LVHW081331050326
832903LV00024B/1120